No Valley Too Deep

No Valley Too Deep

Gloria Hurst

MOODY PRESS
CHICAGO

Second Printing, 1978

Library of Congress Cataloging in Publication Data
Hurst, Gloria, 1928-
    No valley too deep.

    1. Hurst, Gloria, 1928- 2. Christian biography—United States.
3. Divorcees—United States—Biography. I. Title.
BR1725.H855A36   248'.2'0924 [B]   78-6505
ISBN 0-8024-5947-1

The use of selected references from various versions of the Bible in this publication does not necessarily imply publisher endorsement of the versions in their entirety.
Some of the material in this book is taken from "Joy Has Come," by Gloria Hurst, *Decision*, March, 1977, ©1977 by the Billy Graham Evangelistic Association.

Printed in the United States of America

DEDICATION

To Edith Bushi, an "angel";
and to my children—
Tom, David, Karen, Paul,
Mary, Ann, Steven, Peter,
Margaret, Patricia, and Barbara.

"Happy are those who are strong in the Lord, who want above all else to follow your steps. When they walk through the Valley of Weeping it will become a place of springs where pools of blessing and refreshment collect after rains! They will grow constantly in strength and each of them is invited to meet with the Lord in Zion."

Psalm 84:5-7 (TLB)*

*Verses marked TLB are taken from *The Living Bible,* copyright 1971 by Tyndale House Publishers, Wheaton, Ill. Used by permission.

1

Despairing, empty, stripped of all self-esteem—how can I best describe the depth of my feelings on that spring morning?

I had left my six-month-old baby with her father while I drove to the shopping center. I stared at the other shoppers. It was the usual assortment of women you would see in that popular grocery store on any given day.

There were the young, sophisticated housewives who made it a point to appear very chic in the latest fashions. There were the more affluent, established matrons who could afford to stand at the meat counter in seventy-five-dollar pantsuits. I related more to the slightly plump, motherly looking type. Today, they were just a blend of faces.

I tried to study one face after another. If I could see beneath the facade of sophistication and affluence, what would I find?

Does she have a husband who must meet business associates for late dinners? Has she found strange lipstick on her husband's shirt collar?

Where did they find their coping power? In bridge parties with the girls? Perhaps they shared confidences with a friendly beautician.

Was I just an old-fashioned prude? The new morality doesn't object to flirting or an occasional fling for husbands or wives. Why couldn't I bend and adjust to those new standards of morality?

Just the suspicion of another woman in my husband's life was more heartsick pain than I could bear.

The grocery list in my hand gave me some stability. I had a family of thirteen depending on me for the preparation of meals and the other household care. I struggled to locate bread and baby milk. The shelves of food just blurred in front of me. There were no tears, just the inability to concentrate on such mundane details. Desperately, I began to realize that I was failing in the most important area of my life.

The events of the past six months had led me down to a level of despair I had never dreamed possible. I had been a very special person; I was the loved and secure wife of a respectable businessman. For two decades, I had known that my husband loved me as much as I loved him. I had quipped to friends, "I would trust my husband in a *harem!*" Yet there I stood trembling, insecure, almost paranoid, because I felt my world collapsing around me.

A few months earlier I had been invited to join my husband at a dinner for a prospective sales customer. The sales manager and his wife were to be the hosts.

As I combed my fine, unmanageable hair, I hoped Mrs. Sales Manager might not look too chic and trim. My white wool suit was perfect for the cool spring evening, but I regretted at least ten unnecessary pounds. They ruined the sought-after image of a chic, poised young matron.

I did not want to look like the middle-aged mother of eleven children. Outsiders expected me to look frumpy and unkempt. It was bad enough that my husband and I both felt some personal guilt for the current population explosion and its dire forecast of famine and related social problems. Our affluent neighbors were quite content with small families. It was sometimes a question in our minds whether we were recognized as rule-abiding Catholics or felt to be simply two dumb people paying a high price for ignorance in sexual matters. My husband and I both worked hard to destroy the concept of a large family's having to live with mess and clutter.

I was so proud of my husband. He was tall, model slim, and always the perfect gentleman—the essence of good manners and consideration in and out of our home. Now that he was distinguishingly gray-haired, he looked immaculate in his business suits.

That night of the dinner party was somewhat fateful. As I came down the open stairway, he made a perfunctory remark, "You look nice." He barely glanced at me. My sensitive ears picked up the colorless tone. He might just as well have said, "Gloria, you look purple"!

Mrs. Sales Manager looked very trim in a plain black dress. Her hair was cropped in a mannish style. Happily, I noticed that her makeup was no more skillfully applied than mine.

We were seated next to each other during the dinner. While the men chatted enthusiastically about sports or business, she and I exchanged confidences.

She was a very lonely woman. Their only daughter was already in college. Mr. Sales Manager was never at home for the big moments in their daughter's life. Her first date, a special event at school—all the traumatic moments of childhood were all delegated to the mother. I had to acknowledge a truth. My children were getting only fragments of time from their busy father.

On New Year's Eve, my husband suggested we go out to dinner to usher in the new year. It was too late for me to make an appointment with the hairdresser. My dress seemed inappropriate, and the evening seemed dark and cold.

I had always welcomed quiet celebrations with friends or alone with my wonderful husband. Our marriage had improved with age. It was my husband who would announce to visitors, "The honeymoon has never ended." Our little children would try to wiggle between us to enjoy the warmth of our kisses. My love had grown over the years, along with a secure, trusting faith in the man with whom I had chosen to spend the rest of my life.

This gala evening had a heavy sense of foreboding hanging over it. Was it woman's intuition that told me 1970 would be anything but a happy new year for me?

The seeds of anxiety and fear had begun to sprout in my inner spirit.

2

On August 26, 1950, I woke up very early. It was my wedding day! From three or four beaus, I had made my choice. This fellow by the name of Hurst had won the contest hands down. No one could compare to him. We dreamed the same dreams, and we shared the same principles and morals. I had prayed that God would send me a prince, and I was sure my prayers had been answered.

There was a slight mist falling most of the day, but no one seemed to notice, least of all me.

Friends and relatives filled the church to witness the joining of two well-matched people in the bonds of holy matrimony. I walked down the aisle on the arm of my favorite uncle. It was a long and impressive ceremony. As the priest spread his hands over our kneeling forms to offer the nuptial blessing, I felt awed, as if in the presence of almighty God.

There had to be the usual adjustments from the single life. I was very independent, with little thought that perhaps my new partner didn't always read my mind and agree with me.

My in-laws were very close to their son, and they did not relish the idea of someone else's taking first place in his life. There were conflicts of interest until we established a pattern for the harmony we both sincerely yearned for.

Money and material things were scarce. We had trouble finding money for baby shoes. Perhaps that was because we needed so many pairs! In later years we would often laugh at our rapid family growth. We could not possibly have envisioned such fertility, and the prospects were frightening!

In 1952, Thomas Dean gave me a hard labor, but proved to be an enormous asset to our marriage. Tommy was every man's dream of a son. He was "Daddy's boy." He had matching pep, talent, ability, and fun. He was a fabulous source of joy to us as he ran rather than walked through the years. I considered labeling him hyperactive, because his energy had no limit.

He was the first and last child to be rocked to sleep. His keen ears would pick up the squeak of the last floorboard no matter how carefully we tried to step gingerly to his crib.

Tommy invaded all my cupboards. The pots and pans, even the canned goods were constantly spread out on the floor. I often stumbled unaware of an obstacle he had arranged, but his disarming smile spared him many spankings.

Tommy established the pattern of parental care we would use for the rest of our offspring. My husband had been raised to expect a spanking when he misbehaved. Some of his punishments were memorable, such as the time he filled his father's gas tank with sand. I had been raised without spankings, but with severe, caustic disapproval. I personally felt I would have preferred spanking.

As Tom grew older, we were determined to be a praying family. We would hold his tiny hands so he soon learned the prayer before meals. Grandparents who absentmindedly picked up a fork full of food were chagrined to hear their little grandson remind them not to be pagans!

We took Tom to church when he reached the age of four. He had been such an active boy, we were reluctant to attempt it any earlier. Before leaving the house, Tommy was duly instructed to behave. He was to copy our movements. I think we underestimated Tommy. He watched us very carefully, and when I scratched my nose, he scratched his!

In 1954, a second son joined our family. Unlike Tommy, David Robert was very quiet and passive. He was also very affectionate and easy to live with. In later years, it was David who would spend hours playing with the younger ones. Both Tom and David always welcomed the newest arrival. Jealousy was never a problem.

During Lent, the schoolchildren were asked to save pennies for the missions. This was always called "the pagan baby fund." At Easter, my David came home in tears. He had turned in his box of pennies, and the Sister had told him he could not have a "pagan baby"!

In 1956, Tommy and David spread the happy news that the Easter bunny had brought them a baby sister. Karen Elizabeth was a big thrill for all of us. My elated husband nearly did handsprings down the hospital corridor. Karen was such a doll, but her little stomach demanded a bottle every three hours all night long for the first six weeks. I was weary beyond words, but I can't forget our joy at having her in the family.

Paul Andrew arrived just thirteen months later. In another year Mary Ellen was born. By now, Tom and David had a job every afternoon when they arrived home from school; there was always a pile of diapers to fold, and probably some dishes to wash and dry. With three babies in diapers, my energy never quite reached to cover all the tasks.

When I had time to remember my own childhood, my thoughts often centered on the time I spent with my maternal grandmother. Her life was so hard because of a chronically ill husband. He was unable to work for all the years I can remember. It was my grandmother's responsibility to take care of the family. She is remembered by her children for the Christian attitude she brought into their lives.

How difficult and physically taxing it must have been in those days before Social Security benefits for the disabled. My grandmother took in nine washings a week to support her five children. They were done on a scrub board with hot water that steamed in a copper boiler on the kerosene cooking stove. Water had to be brought into the house from an outside well that was known to freeze in the winter. The oldest son and daughter left school at an early age to deliver the stacks of neatly washed and ironed laundry in a coaster wagon.

Besides the daily tasks of cleaning, ironing, and cooking, Grandma maintained two half-acre plots of garden. She would be down in the garden at five in the morning. I can vividly remember the fierce attacks of her hoe on the invading weeds. Every fall there were rows and rows of canning jars on shelves in the cellar under the kitchen floor. There were huge crocks of sauerkraut and pickles—mute testimony to her diligence. Where did all that energy and strength come from?

While my mother went off to work every day, I was left in the tender loving care of an aunt, two uncles, and Grandma Steinhorst. This Christian grandmother had such a tremendous impact on my life. She was responsible for teaching me the basics. I don't mean reading and writing. I mean the basic elements we all need to survive in this life and for all eternity.

I never heard my grandmother complain. I heard her pray and sing the old hymns of faith, and I saw her read her Bible for strength. I can remember her on Sunday afternoons. She would open her worn German Bible, and if I was restless, she would let down her long hair so I could comb it.

My grandmother taught me the value of hard work and dedication to a job. She also instilled in me an understanding of the importance of God in my daily life. I suppose that during those lean depression years, many families remembered to thank God for the food on the table. I have rarely eaten a meal without prayer.

Undoubtedly, this heritage sustained me when I might have felt justified in feeling sorry for myself. I had left college to marry. Now it seemed like I was getting a degree in the three Ds—Dishes, Dust, and Diapers! That was before the movement to liberate women from household tasks. I was at home taking care of my babies like millions of women. We felt that was our primary responsibility. Our hard-working parents had encouraged us to work equally hard for the things we wanted out of life. I wonder what small seeds am I planting now for my children to harvest in their adult years.

Ann Marie arrived in 1959, just a year after Mary Ellen. Mary had such straight black hair, and Ann Marie had blond curls encircling her face like a cherub.

A year after Ann, we welcomed Steven John. Here again was the boundless energy we had first seen in Tom. Peter Damien arrived a year later. Like David, Peter endured hours of teasing from Tom and Steven.

By now we had outgrown the conventional table and chairs. My creative husband decided we would cover a door with formica, and then he built a long, sturdy bench for each side. It seemed to me that this prince of mine could do just about anything for us. My children could not have picked a better father.

My husband was as helpful as any young father could be. At bath time he would kneel over the tub with his shirt sleeves rolled up and bathe two babies at a time. The room was filled with giggles as he washed between small toes with a large finger. Even shampoos were not too much of a challenge for him. As each baby was washed, I took it into my arms to be dried and dressed in pajamas. It was really assembly-line efficiency.

We couldn't often afford a baby-sitter, but we didn't feel deprived. It was romantic to splurge on a piece of steak and share it by candlelight when the last baby was fed and asleep. These were quiet, intimate moments to share only with each other. Deep thoughts were revealed and dreams unfolded.

In the fall of 1963, my husband began to feel very discontented with his job. There were personality conflicts that upset both of us. By now, my husband had risen to the position of sales manager in the company. He was gone on week-long sales trips. He was fast becoming an expert in the field of human relations. He handled fellow sales people and irate customers with equal ease. I was proud of his honesty, integrity, and ambition.

When he announced he wanted to take a new position in faraway Michigan, it never occurred to me to object to leaving our hometown. In my devotion, and with confidence, I would have agreed to Alaska or Timbuktu.

Suddenly, this immature and unsophisticated housewife was thrust into the world of suburbia. My clothes, my hair, and perhaps even my face needed to change.

We always had financial struggles, but then, what

16

young couple doesn't? It was a delight to notice one factor. My young executive husband would receive a raise or a promotion within months of the birth of the latest child. We laughingly suggested that we couldn't really afford to stop having children.

All our friends in suburbia were purchasing appliances on the time payment plan just as we were. Some were overdoing their debts in a mad passion to keep up with the Joneses. Everyone on the block was measured by the quantity and quality of his material possessions.

It wasn't long before we became a two-car family. Now we were definitely on the upward climb. I became more adept at social functions and a bit more self-confident as time went on.

Away from our families, we were more determined to find security close to God. Several of our children had made their first communion, and even the confirmation rite. We took counsel and advice from the priests quite willingly. We didn't argue when they advised us to tithe. Our scrupulous consciences made us obedient to God out of *fear* and respect if not out of love for Him. As we prospered, we felt we were being rewarded for our obedience.

In 1964, our family moved again. My husband was offered a better opportunity to grow in his line of work, and the financial rewards were too tempting to resist. The new job meant we would live in Ohio. I had some minor misgivings. I had a real fear of flying. My husband had shared some of his bad experiences with me, and I experienced real anxiety for his safety whenever business required him to fly. My family was back in Wisconsin. If there should be an emergency, I might have to travel by plane to save time. I tried to push these thoughts back, because the most important thing was to be with my husband wherever his work might be.

Our youngest daughter so far, Margaret Mary, had been born in Wisconsin. She was now old enough to walk through the big, old, brick house we purchased in Ohio. The bungalow style would lend itself to the extensive remodeling plans we drew. Eventually, the house grew to eight bedrooms and three and a half baths. I had a full-time job of child care and housework.

I realize most women would recoil in horror at the mere thought of such a life of housework and confinement. Perhaps I would have rejected the idea of a large family and its responsibilities if I had not felt the total love and support of my husband. Also, we were a devout Catholic family. We had received rigid instructions concerning our responsibilities in the married state. We followed all the rules.

In the long months of pregnancy, I would often pray for strength to overcome the waves of nausea and weakness. I could endure the difficult time only because I was confident I would deliver a beautiful and healthy baby. My uterine muscles remained in top condition. I didn't even develop varicose veins in my legs. Surely, I reasoned, God must be partially satisfied with my attempts to live up to the rules set forth by the Roman Catholic Church.

After the new baby came home, there were sleepless nights of changing diapers and warming bottles for the hungry infant. The priests were not entirely without sympathy. More than one expressed admiration for the mothers who tended large families, and the fathers who willingly assumed such heavy responsibilities. Frequently we were advised to "offer up" our pains and problems.

As I awoke to the baby's cry, I would take a moment

to sit on the edge of the bed. I would bow my head and say, "All for You, dear Jesus." Surely, He knew that my stitches were pulling and painful. He knew pain and weariness in His brief life on this earth. He would sympathize with me.

The Catholic church didn't relax the rules until after Vatican II. By then our family had increased. Patricia Kay was born in 1965. Barbara Ann joined us in 1968.

The grand total was now eleven children, a collie, a cat, and various wildlife Steven rescued from the lawn mower. It was a full house, but our three acres, our thirteen-room house, and our hearts all seemed adequate to the task. There was an abundance of comfort and happiness.

I had been an only child. Growing up in the years just after the terrible depression of the thirties, I had had a real shortage of playmates. Now I was never lonely. I would watch the children at play, and even when there was a squabble, I would think, *Well, at least you have someone to fight with!*

My children seemed to enjoy being together. Almost every night there was a fast kick-ball game in the big driveway. A few neighbor children might join in the teams. It was a fun time for everyone.

3

Our children required hospitalization just twice in eighteen years. The doctor bills were unbelievably small. The milk bill was enormous, but the dentist never got rich from our family.

Our apparent good fortune began to concern me. It just didn't seem possible that we should escape all the misfortune of life. People all around us were experiencing problems with illness or finances. Why were we spared, and for how long? I began to pray that God would give me the strength for these problems when they did come. By now, we were approaching middle age, when women had operations and husbands had heart attacks.

My husband's business was good, and continually growing. Now we could finally afford some of the extras we had denied ourselves for so many years. There were two new Chryslers in our garage and new furniture in the house.

After the house was all remodeled, we added a beautiful in-the-ground pool. This wasn't so much a luxury as it was a necessity every summer. I had eleven bored children once school was out. Most of them were too young for jobs, with the exception of a paper route. You can only spend so much time at the library and still get the household tasks finished. It was a lovely pool with a curved slide and a jump board. Even the youngest became quite a water baby.

My husband had become more and more precious to me through the years. I began the day by planning for him—his favorite meal, a special dessert, anything to please him. Our day began when he came home from his sales trips. Our lives seemed to revolve around his activities in the house or the yard. The family followed him as he mowed the lawn on the tractor. The little ones got to ride on his lap. If my husband was sawing lumber in the basement or doing some rewiring, most of us were by his side.

I was convinced I had a perfect husband, and for him I would be the perfect wife and mother. I was very proud of my family. I saw my children as real masterpieces. I suppose most mothers feel that way, but I was sure I was being quite objective.

Their father insisted on adult manners. Many grown-ups were startled to see our young sons extend their hands for a shake on the occasion of an introduction. They stood up when older people entered the room. These formal niceties were beginning to fade from our culture.

One evening my husband arrived home early from a sales trip. Abruptly, he announced, "I've decided to open up a sales office downtown."

We had always discussed even the purchase of a small appliance. Opening an office downtown was a major step and certainly an expensive venture. My thoughts were only momentary questions, because I had no reason to doubt his judgment. He had certainly proved himself to be a good provider. I felt just a twinge of regret that we had not made this plan together. It was the first time I felt I was a *lesser* partner in our marriage.

The small basement office was inexpensive and

tax-deductible. It had been an economic necessity when my husband began his work as a manufacturer's representative. I couldn't argue; we had progressed to a point where it would be convenient for him to have a formal office downtown.

As before, I continued to save and sew and cut corners until we had accumulated the thousands of dollars this venture required. The entire family was proud of a successful Dad.

The work load we carried at home and in the office was heavy.

Quite honestly, we both became workaholics! I had so many household tasks, I had to budget my time very carefully. My husband was so tied to his office phone that he would never leave the office early for fear he would miss a new order. The tension and pressure of that kind of life took a toll on us.

I began to plead for a vacation. Our honeymoon had been just three rainy days in northern Wisconsin. Now we lived so close to Niagara Falls. Better yet, I'd like to see Hawaii! So it was agreed, we would have a second honeymoon in Hawaii for our twentieth wedding anniversary. Just two years to wait. For his birthday in September, I bought a new suitcase and filled it with travel folders of the islands. There were fun and excitement just ahead for us.

My husband opened his new office. Then there were even more nights away from home. I had less and less contact with his world of business. The business mail didn't come to the house anymore. The letterheads had all become familiar—like friends.

I began to notice little things that only a wife could register because of the closeness of a marriage relationship.

He was eager to leave for work in the morning, but his steps dragged in the evening as I waited for him to come in from the garage. He was too quiet. When I asked, "What's new in the outside world?" he would shrug his shoulders and find a newspaper to bury his head.

I began to find magazine articles about the problems in marriages that had lasted as long as ours. They said the excitement was all gone. There was nothing new in the relationship. Surely, they were talking about *other* couples.

The texture of my homemade bread became super-fine as I kneaded and pounded out my frustrations.

The children began to notice that Daddy wasn't interested in the kick-ball game anymore. Sunday afternoons he would nap on the living room floor. I began to feel alone in a house full of people.

Finally my husband and I began to play a game at bedtime. The object was to see who could get to bed first and pretend to be asleep before the other.

There was less and less communication between us. Even the kisses of greeting or good-bye seemed a heavy obligation for him. Occasionally I would tease, "Do you still love me?" He'd reply, "Of course!" and smile reassuringly. I wondered if it was the heavy pressure of his business, or something else. It couldn't be *someone* else—no, never.

After a few months, I began to experience real nightmares. They were more than bad dreams, because I was wide awake! They were hour-long sessions filled with fear and anxiety.

One night I tapped him on the shoulder to tell him my worst fears. He rolled over and listened, but there was no word or sign of compassion from him. I tearfully spilled out my feelings.

When I told him I felt he no longer loved me, he became very abrupt. The very idea was more ridiculous than when I woke him to listen to some strange noise in the night.

"I wonder what you will imagine next," was his reply. He rolled back over on his side and was quiet. I was stunned.

This wasn't the same tender, compassionate man who previously would have cradled me in his arms and reassured me of his love. I had known an adoring husband who would wrap me in his arms and lovingly declare that he loved me so much he could hardly bear it.

How could I live without this intimacy? Where else could one find release from the pressure and tension that accrued just from daily life? Surely we were both bruised by daily encounters with thoughtless people and fearful circumstances. Always, in the quiet of the bedroom, we could find a mutual healing and refreshment in the surrendering of our bodies to each other. Confessing our love and need for each other had therapeutic value for both of us. Now for months I had sensed this coldness and unpenetrable distance between us.

I barely recognized my name. It sounded so strange. Who was *Gloria*? I had been accustomed to answering to "Honey," or "Darling." Now he was calling me "Gloria."

I had heard about middle-age problems for women. I could be having hormone problems that cause depression and other unexplained emotions. It seemed reasonable to me that the mother of eleven children couldn't escape without a big dose of *everything*. I was too miserable to ignore the problem.

I made an appointment with my gynecologist for a complete checkup. If I was imagining my problems, I would need medical help before I became a burden to my husband and the children.

After the checkup, my doctor sat across from me at his desk. He had delivered my last two babies, and I felt comfortable as I confided in him. It was hard to keep the tears back as I confessed a deep sadness.

I reminded him that he had given me some little white pills after Barbie was born. I had had a mild depression, and the pills had cured my "third day blues," as he called it.

He reached over and took my hands in his. If I felt that depressed, he would advise me to see a psychiatrist. That didn't arouse anger or resentment in me. I had planned to see a psychiatrist on my own if I didn't get the little white pills from the gynecologist. I was too miserable to go on without professional help, and I knew it all too well.

He wrote down the name of a very good doctor who could help me. This wasn't a hormone condition brought on by middle age. That news was only small comfort. I must be on the road to insanity to imagine my husband could leave me and our beautiful children for any reason. I must be the reason for the estrangement.

My innermost feelings were in constant conflict. Insecurity and doubts about myself were my constant companions.

One day early in spring, it was warm enough to put a coat of paint on the weatherworn bathhouse.

It wasn't unusual for me to tackle this kind of job. I had nailed subflooring and smoothed cement. Now my husband was so tied to his office, even with a full-time secretary, he had little or no time for these projects.

Just before noon, when the sun was high and the temperature the hottest, my husband surprised me by driving into the yard. It was just a quick stop to pick up some papers from the basement office.

Every day, I carefully arranged my time to include a shower and fresh makeup before this special man came home. Now, here I stood, splattered with paint, dripping with perspiration, wearing my oldest grubby clothes.

I waved a greeting from the backyard. He walked back to see the paint job—and me. What a contrast I must have been to the well-groomed woman waiting back in the air-conditioned office.

I felt absolutely sick. I felt defeated.

4

The psychiatrist was very gracious, kind, and understanding. She wasn't at all what I expected. I look back with a smile. I made some very abrupt statements on that first visit. I wonder what kind of an impression I made.

I started out with the intense declaration that while I respected her amount of training and her intelligence, I feared she would try to convince me prayer had no value. I felt these well-trained people depended on science to prove all things. God is a Spirit, and like the wind. We cannot see the wind, only its results as it bends a tree.

I was having a great deal of difficulty praying, in my state of mind, but I wanted to retain the faith I had. God had always been important to me, and I never believed I could make it through life without Him.

The doctor hastened to tell me that she and her family attended church and she too believed in prayer. I began to relax. I sensed her genuine concern for me.

The appointments were two weeks apart, or oftener if I felt particularly troubled. Unfortunately, since my problem didn't go away, the amount of pills and capsules increased. The pain of rejection and depression increased at a steady rate. I was taking muscle relaxers, antidepressants, tranquilizers, and sleeping pills. All of these were meant to relieve my growing depression and make my life tolerable. I went through the days like a robot.

The doctor was becoming increasingly annoyed with me. I kept insisting I had no reason to feel such despair. I repeated the same phrases over and over on each visit. "I have a loving husband and beautiful children."

One day she stood up and flung down her notebook. "When are you going to face the truth? Your husband is unfaithful!"

I went to the car. It was a half-hour later before I could turn on the ignition and put the car into reverse. I was frozen with inner turmoil. How could I survive if she was telling me the truth? My husband could live without me, but I could never live without him. The doctor didn't know my husband. She didn't know the kind of man I had married. He could never forget how much we all loved him. Our hearts ached with loneliness when he left on a business trip. Now this doctor was telling me he didn't need me. He was seeking companionship with someone else.

That had to be untrue. I didn't reveal her words to anyone. She could be mistaken.

By the end of June, after months of coolness, my husband admitted that my worst fears were not just wild imaginations of a sick mind. Now there was no longer any pretense of a warm relationship. I realized I had better prepare the children for their father's next move—out of our home, into a rooming house.

Strangely, I was calm and tearless as I told Tom and the others. My oldest son didn't have the calming effect of a tranquilizer, and he burst forth in grief, disbelief, and then anger. He made a fist and struck the wall. I followed him out to the garage, where his father was getting ready to leave for the office.

28

"Dad, you can't do this! You'll burn for it!"

Suddenly, the car squealed around the curve and down the long driveway. A very angry man was at the wheel. He was furious with me for telling our son that there was another woman. I stood speechless and dumb.

My son was in painful anguish, and my husband was distraught beyond words. How could anyone make peace in our home after all this? There would be no celebration on July 4, 1970.

In less than two weeks, my husband packed his things and moved into a rooming house. He visited the children on weekends. His comments to me always were brief.

"Is everything all right?"

My reply was automatic. "Sure, everything is fine." It was unthinkable to whine or complain in front of the children. We had always solved our differences in private.

Occasionally he would stay for lunch, to the delight of the entire family. We chattered like magpies, and the visit would always end too soon for us.

I lived in a sedated stupor to bear the pain for myself and my children. I could not stop crying. Concerned friends and relatives assured me that this difficulty would work itself out in time. But time was not healing me. The days dragged by, yet they were all a blur through my drugged condition. The summer ended, and then it was fall and then winter. Preparation for Christmas took all my strength. Only a sense of obligation kept me going.

There was no change in our relationship when spring appeared on the calendar. By the end of April, I was too miserable to go on. I made an appointment with the doctor, and pleaded to be hospitalized.

My husband drove me to the hospital on a Monday

morning. He carried my suitcase into the psychiatric ward. It didn't concern me that the door was locked behind me. I had nowhere to go on this day in May 1971.

As I looked around me, I wondered if I had a right to be there. The other patients looked very sick. Perhaps I was taking a bed away from someone who really needed it! Compassion for the other patients was my only concern.

The doctor smiled at me. "Gloria, you are sick too!"

Who could argue with that? I felt sick!

I was given a heavy dose of insulin every other day. I was grateful, because the electric shock treatments had such devastating aftereffects on the other patients.

After the first two weeks, I came home for a weekend visit. Steven met me at the door.

"Mom, you were only going to be gone a week!"

It was a scolding given in the sweet love of a child. How could he know my pain? I hugged him to hide my tears. All the children had had a difficult time while I was gone, but I was glad to go back to the rest and quiet of the ward. My fifteen-year-old daughter had to assume the role of mother.

I was in the hospital on Mother's Day. My husband came with a dozen red roses, but they held no special significance for me. Occasionally, he would come to the hospital early to have supper with me in the cafeteria. We didn't have much to say.

Only the nurse that accompanied the doctor on his rounds heard me spill out my despair. Alice was a beautiful Christian, and she did her best to help me. We took long walks on the grounds for fresh-air therapy.

"Just take one day at a time," she would urge me wisely.

I kept silent most of the time. I had thoughts about the weather or maybe the flowers, but surely my thoughts had no value.

The days were a blessed blur. During each of his visits, I looked for some sign of change in my husband. Surely, he would see our desperate need for him. I had trouble expressing myself vocally, but I often reached for his hand. A firm grasp of his hand might have rescued me from the terrible waves of despair. He withdrew, as if repelled by my existence.

I withdrew from the world. If it was difficult to speak, it was equally hard to write or read.

Television was boring, but it was our only pastime. We lost our problems in the game shows and in the antics of Flip Wilson's characterization of Geraldine. I refused to watch the soap operas. The plots were too similar to my real-life scenes!

After six weeks, I left the hospital. The adjustment back to a normal household routine was almost too much for me. It was like going from the frying pan into the fire. I could barely tolerate the pressures of home. There was a continual clamor for my attention and service. "What should I wear?" and "What's for supper?" My sweet children seemed totally self-centered and demanding.

My husband had moved back into our house while I was hospitalized, but he carefully avoided giving me the notion that he had any special feeling for me. He would only speak to me when it was coldly impersonal. Finally, it was too difficult, and he left again.

The swimming pool offered me a means of escape. I would float on my back and watch the cloud formations. The water therapy was a great supplement to the myriad of pills and capsules. The doctor teased, "We'll have to chip off the ice in winter."

Within a month of my homecoming, there was a

somber-faced policeman at the door. He asked if I was Paul's mother. Cold fear gripped me.

Paul had been hit by a car as he crossed the road on his bike on the afternoon paper route.

God, I really don't need this, I protested.

Fortunately, David was at home to drive us to the emergency room. I had no idea how to reach my husband while he was out on a sales call. The answering service was not much help. As David drove, I trembled uncontrollably. Every nerve ending was protesting.

By the time we got to the emergency room, Paul was being wheeled out of the X-ray room. The attendant reported that Paul would have to spend the night for observation. He would be all right. He had escaped with minor cuts and bruises.

Finally, the summer ended, and I felt some relief having the children in school all day. However, the teachers called me repeatedly for conferences. Everyone was doing so poorly, and no one could understand it. The children passed on to the next grade with a long list of incompletes on their report cards.

The children were all sensitive to my pain and responded in their own ways. Patty would suggest that I bake a pie when she observed me sitting by the window too still and too long. She would cry every afternoon as the school bus came to take her to kindergarten. She was afraid I wouldn't be home when she returned. That was far too much pain for one so young.

A young son began to wet the bed and talk in his sleep. He was terribly embarrassed, but he couldn't control his reaction.

The weekends were the worst. We were all bored and extremely lonely. There was no dad to watch with some project. No dad to instruct or counsel. We would roam through the nearby department store for an inexpensive form of diversion.

On Saturday nights, my oldest daughters hurried off to babysitting jobs. That left me alone with my youngest children. It took all my energy to supervise their baths and get them off to bed. All my incentive was gone. I was going to bed by eight-thirty myself, just to escape. My mind was too clouded for handiwork or a book. At times I was overwhelmed with self-pity. Would I be destined to spend all my hours alone for the rest of my life? As in my lonely teenage years, I agonized, "Does anyone love me?" There was no answer in the quiet, dark room.

I desperately needed to feel like a person again.

One day, my eyes fell on a newspaper ad. There would be a short charm course at one of the large department stores. That was interesting. I had experienced quite a weight loss, and now I felt like continuing with improvements toward becoming a new Gloria.

We had a vibrant teacher in her fifties. Her personality and energy would never have betrayed her age. Once I had had such a zest for life. Could I recapture it?

Each week there were classes on exercise, dress styles to flatter, and then a session on hair styling. Each of us received personal attention. I was intrigued when the teacher suggested I lighten my hair. I made an appointment to have it done. Would my husband notice I had become a blond? Would he be pleased and interested? I kept hoping for a miracle.

By October another ugly trouble reared its head. My thirteen-year-old daughter began to display some disturbing signs of depression.

One afternoon I went to find her for the evening meal. She was sitting at the far end of our lot in an old cemetery. She had her arms around an old tombstone

33

that bore her first name. When I urged her to come with me for dinner, she stubbornly refused to leave. "It's peaceful here, and I'm not hungry," she insisted.

I fed the younger children and then hurried back to where Mary still sat. Suddenly her mood changed, and she wanted to walk up and down the driveway, chattering incessantly. Finally, we were both exhausted, and she agreed to go to her room and rest.

I made sure she was quieted, and then I ran down to the basement extension phone for a call to my doctor. She agreed that Mary should be closely watched for a time.

Two days later, Mary staggered down to breakfast. She was whining and complaining of not feeling well. When I probed, "Why don't you feel well?" she admitted she had tried to swallow two dozen aspirins.

I placed another frantic phone call to the doctor. It was important to get Mary to the emergency room as soon as possible. It was already too late to pump her stomach, but intravenous feeding might prevent kidney damage. Her acidity count was up 50 percent. There was a continual buzzing in her head.

I felt heartsick as I visited my beautiful Mary behind the locked door of the same psychiatric ward where I had spent six weeks. I put on a mask of cheerfulness to hide my thoughts from her. She didn't feel loved, and she didn't want to come home. All the same sick emotions I had had to deal with and live with.

After five weeks, Mary was ready to come home. In another week she was ready to go back to school on just a small amount of medication. She had managed to get through the days better than I.

After I had come home from the hospital, it was difficult for me to get dressed for church on Sunday. I didn't attend Mass for several weeks. For the first time in my life, I didn't care if I went to church. It just didn't matter.

As a child, I had broken out with measles one Sunday morning. Frantic, I begged my mother to rub my face with alcohol so the rash would fade and I could still go to Sunday school. I *had* to have perfect attendance no matter what.

Occasionally, a small son might be bold enough to venture, "Is there really a God?"

We would hush him with a stern voice. "Of course there is a God." Such doubts were a terrible sin, and we hoped even God hadn't heard the question! We didn't dare admit that as adults we had questions. Now I freely wondered, *Could it be that the concept of God was designed by people who recognized we needed a basis for a moral code in our civilizations?*

I had always been reduced to tears when I followed the priest around during the Stations of the Cross. Christ's agony and humiliation were vividly impressed upon me.

I was sincerely devout as the priest elevated the eucharist during the communion portion of the Mass. I repeated the words of Thomas, "My Lord and my God." I generated this spirituality, but I sincerely wanted to know there was a God. All this served me well until trouble came, and then it was obviously not enough. Doctrine had not lifted my despair. The clergy could sympathize, but they didn't have any answers for a marriage in trouble.

Organized religion *talked* love and brotherhood, but I saw people leave the services and literally fight for their right to be the first out of the parking lot. I didn't feel I had any brothers or sisters. Close friends were scarce. Organized religion was empty of the precepts I associated with God. God may have been inside the church for me, but He didn't come outside to have any special relationship with me.

In the recesses of my mind were memories of the early Sunday-school training I had received. We had learned the little song with a big meaning, "Jesus Loves Me." Perhaps truth and love could still be found in the Bible.

A very concerned aunt sent me a small booklet of Scripture verses designed to help the despairing soul as a spiritual vitamin. I began to read the verses, and then I reread them, because there was strength in those lines. I gave up the newspaper at breakfast. My reading rate was very slow, and my comprehension not much faster, so I was not bored.

One day a new friend suggested I join her for a neighborhood Bible study. Perhaps more Scripture was what I needed!

I was introduced to about eight other women. After the friendly greetings were over, we seated ourselves around a large dining room table.

I felt slightly uncomfortable. How much did they know about me and my problems? But their welcome was so warm, it was only a short time before I entered into the reading and discussion.

We used a lesson book that repeated the life and death of Jesus Christ as I had known it from a child. These kindly ladies were obviously concerned for me. They urged me to begin to read the Bible every day. I wasn't sure I could share their enthusiasm. I had a lovely, big, family Bible, but I couldn't ever get interested enough to read it for any length of time. I read the Christmas story to my children, and I enjoyed the poetry of the Twenty-third Psalm.

After the Bible study, my friend Edith Bushi drove me back home. A shroud of sadness always hung over me, and Edith did her best to offer me comfort.

Genuine love and concern were in her voice. There was a light in her eyes that I had never seen in anyone before.

As we sat in the car she asked me, "Do you know Jesus as your personal Savior?"

"Well," I offered, "I know that Jesus died for the sins of the world."

She wasn't satisfied with my answer. "Are you born again?"

That was totally foreign to me. Was I some kind of second-class Christian after all my years of church attendance? I had certainly been as much of a believer as Edith was! With some degree of indignation and a struggle to be polite, I answered her in the only possible way. I just didn't know what she was trying to get me to say! I never heard the term *born again* in any church I ever attended.

Edith didn't pursue the matter, perhaps sensing she wasn't making any progress with me. But she had planted a seed. My soul was like thirsty soil searching for relief from a drought.

Each day was harder to face than the previous one, and I had to take at least one sleeping pill every night.

One night in April 1972, I reached the absolute limit of my endurance. A full bottle of sleeping pills was on the table beside my bed. I couldn't face another day. The pills didn't ease my pain. My husband was flattered that I would take him back, but he wasn't interested. I was determined not to go back to the hospital.

I lay back on the bed. I smoothed the sheet and then the blanket. These small wrinkles were bothersome, like all the details of my life. Everything was imperfect, and I had had enough of pain.

During my lifetime of religious training, I had been taught that suicide was a sure road to hell. My sick mind reasoned that I would merely be exchanging one hell here in this life for another hell somewhere beyond this existence. The good life I had known was all gone for me. All incentive and desire had drained from me until I felt like an empty shell.

Communication between God and me had broken down. If people didn't understand my pain, perhaps God didn't either. I couldn't see any reason for going on in this constant pain.

There were no light and love in the corners of my room or in any area of my heart.

I looked up at the dark ceiling.

Slowly I began, "God, before I swallow all those pills, I want to know, do You really hear me? Are You a merciful, loving God who hates to see me suffer like this? Have You rejected me like my husband has? *If* You are there, and *if* You love me, oh God, be merciful, and let me die. Take me out of this hell."

I had said my piece to God; *if* there was a God.

Suddenly, God was speaking to me!

Gloria, I accept you, but not to die. You must live.

Almighty God had spoken with such intensity and power, there was no room for doubt. I fell into a deep sleep until morning.

5

When I opened my eyes on April 24, 1972, it was as if a window shade had been lifted. The cloudy veil had been removed from my eyes. My heart was overflowing with God's light and love. He let me see beauty in each of His creations. I saw the true color of every flower. I saw the intricate design of each petal and leaf with the clarity no human biologist could ever impart to his student. Best of all, there was a new love in my heart for each beautiful child in my own home. Now I could finally return the generous love they had unselfishly poured out to me for two dark years.

I saw their tremendous need for me. My baby was very young, and the others were all quite deserving. A new cord of closeness drew each young heart to mine in the power of God's love.

The excitement of this new revelation was too great to keep to myself. As a teenager I had had happy times that made me want to dance and sing my way down the sidewalk. It was hardly proper for me to do such things now, but that is similar to how I felt. Whom could I tell? Who would understand this exuberance I felt in my total being?

My dear friend, Edith Bushi! She would know what joy had come into my life.

Suddenly, I knew the source of that radiant light in

her eyes. She didn't need special eye makeup to look beautiful. Even her laughter had a special lilt to it.

I forgot how very early it was, and I dialed Edith's number. A sleepy voice answered the phone.

I don't remember the exact way I told Edith about the miracle of the previous night. I'm not sure I was at all coherent! My exuberance often shows in bubbles of joy that result in unfinished sentences and expressive exclamations.

Although I may have stumbled through the description, Edith understood and rejoiced with the angels. The change in me was dramatic, and my dear friend has never doubted me.

I'm not surprised when people question the authenticity of someone's actually hearing God's voice. We have been conditioned to look for logic and reason. Such a phenomenon is likely the product of an overactive imagination, experts contend. I agree, it would take an imagination of extraordinary capacity to come up with an experience like mine. However, I was at the point of no talent, no creativity, and certainly no imagination.

Did God speak to the boy Samuel? Did God speak to a lowly shepherd named Amos? Why couldn't a housewife hear Him?

A suspicious deacon asked, "Could it have been the voice of Satan?"

The evil one would certainly have had something to rejoice about if I had swallowed the sleeping pills. My family would have disintegrated, and I would have spent eternity in hell.

Only God gives life, and through Jesus comes a *new* life. With the divine command to live came a full understanding that I had been given an eternal life through Jesus Christ.

I can't explain such mysteries. We will all have questions to ask, unless of course they will no longer be of any concern in the joy of heaven.

Edith explained that when I called on God and asked Him to take charge of my life, I became a born-again creature according to Scripture found in 2 Corinthians 5:17.

"Therefore if any man be in Christ, he is a new creature: old things are passed away; behold, all things are become new."

While I was bursting to share my testimony with everyone, I was the most concerned with my doctor's reaction. What would she say if I told her I didn't need those fourteen pills every day? In fact, I didn't need any pills at all! I hadn't taken any medication for three weeks.

I didn't enjoy scoldings, and a scolding was what I expected. It was probably even dangerous to go off so much medication overnight. Undoubtedly, she would notice I had stopped crying. I was singing through all the household tasks, even trying my hand at baking and sewing again!

She was such a keen observer, I couldn't hide my exhilaration from her, and so I didn't even try. Her only comment was that she hoped I wasn't going to be some religious fanatic who shunned all medicine. She noted that my illness and pain required medication as much as that of a patient with an ailing heart.

One Saturday morning, my husband came to see the children. How I yearned to share this beautiful experience with him. I envisioned how Jesus could lift him above the tension and pressure of the business world. I wanted him to have the same joy in his spirit as the Lord had given me. He did notice I had undergone some kind of change.

I ran down to the mailbox like a schoolgirl going to her first party. I called to him to wait for me as I ran back down the long driveway. He studied me curiously. "Did the doctor give you some new medicine?"

I answered, "No, I'm on the wings of the eagle!"

That answer startled me. I had only heard Isaiah 40:31 once or twice. Now it took on a special meaning to me. I was definitely on the wings of the eagle! I could tell from the look in this man's eyes that he wasn't understanding me.

"Well, whatever it is, I'm glad you're feeling better."

I could hardly wait to get into my new modern version of the Bible. There were scores of promises for the weak to be strengthened. It was exciting and fascinating, because the message was always so personal. The Bible was not just a book anymore. It was my own special treasure.

God literally moved into our house. He was so real, I saw Him in everything, and then I expressed my thoughts to the children.

Of course, the children couldn't help but notice my changed attitude. How they must have suffered when I was praying to die! Now the Holy Spirit was using me to teach my children and show them the way to the rich life He could provide.

It took only two weeks for thirteen-year-old Mary to approach me. Mary had certainly gone through a personal hell of her own. She was still taking medication to ease her pain and help her function in school. It had been a hard winter for both of us. Now she wanted to know why I had stopped crying. I began with eagerness.

She had no trouble understanding my account of my suicide plans, but when I told her that God had spoken to me, Mary bolted and ran. I could hear her sobbing as she made her way up the stairs.

What had I done but add to her burden and unhappiness! I prayed that God would give me a second chance.

About a week later, Mary came to me with an apology.

"I'm sorry, Mom; I really want to hear all about you and God." She went on to explain that she was jealous because God had helped me and she had had no relief.

With a new prayer for guidance, I began to share with Mary a second time.

Just outside the back door was a lovely new flower. Very slowly, I explained how the flower accepted all things from God without question. The rain washed and refreshed the flower. The sunshine gave new life and vitality. At night the petals closed and the flower rested.

I explained to Mary that I would live my life as God directed. I would give up my own will and trust God for my life day by day.

I honestly feel that the Holy Spirit directed that simple explanation, because Mary burst into a beautiful smile of understanding. Tears of joy flowed down our cheeks as we embraced in a new love. We both had much to learn, but it was a start. Time would teach us the full meaning of our divine encounter.

Mary became a beautiful Christian teenager. She started a Bible study at high school during the noon hour. Several students found a new relationship with Christ through her efforts. She never minded being called a Jesus freak.

Paul returned home from Boy Scout camp to view all the changes. We had happiness for breakfast, dinner, and supper these days. The problems hadn't gone away, but we were handling them differently. There were smiles and jokes again. There were also Scripture verses posted on the refrigerator door every day.

Paul couldn't help but notice how his mother had

changed. After a few days, he pulled me aside for a serious talk. We smile now as we remember his utmost sincerity.

"Mom, if I didn't know you better, I'd think you had been drinking!" We both knew I was a poor social drinker, usually selecting only the cocktail most resembling lemonade when social pressure made selection necessary. It wasn't alcohol that flowed in my veins!

When Mary had come to ask me the source of my joy, I was poorly equipped to speak on the subject of a new life in Jesus Christ. In fact, I did such a poor job, she had had to come to me a second time. I had the zeal and enthusiasm of all newborn Christians, but I lacked wisdom. As Paul waited, I was grateful for the Bible study lessons of the past months. Now, I was equipped to lead all my children to a saving knowledge of Jesus. Paul had seen me bubble with the joy of Jesus, and he was open to any advice I might have so he could enjoy this new life with Mary and me. I explained that conversion doesn't require a suicidal experience but an openness to realize man is a sinner by nature. I told Paul that he must recognize his inability to redeem himself, and believe that Jesus Christ is the one who died to save Paul Hurst. It had to be a personal decision for Paul.

My son could not resist the strong evidence of a renewed life in his mother. He had gone away to camp that summer still believing he was losing the mother he loved. Now the same mother was a different person. Paul decided that he too needed a change in his life. Karen and Steven made the same decision in a short time.

Jesus became so real, I was surprised the girls didn't set a place at the table for Him at mealtime.

My youngest girls, Patty and Barbie, learned that

Jesus loved them. They began to attend Sunday school at the Parma Heights Baptist Church, where they quickly grasped the evangelical precepts. Barbie began to check up on all visitors. Even the milkman got the security check. She'd pull me aside to whisper, "Do they have Jesus in their hearts?" She wasn't three years old, but she recognized the new importance we gave to God. Young children are open to the love of God.

I was surprised at how much our family was enjoying church. Previously, it was an obligation to attend, and it was a heavy one for most of the children. They wiggled and fussed through the short half-hour services. Now we were going to church three times a week!

Prayer became a joy. God wasn't fearsome or far away. He was a friend that we could talk to about anything. He didn't laugh or think me foolish when I failed. I was still slow and weak, so I often prayed for strength and more time to finish the housework. My checkbook was a source of concern. Math had never been one of my strong points, and often I would panic in the confusion.

Every activity was given over to the Lord. When we approached the intersection and the light suddenly turned green, we'd wave a thank you to the Lord. We felt He was watching over us. Every time we rode in the car, we sang familiar hymns or choruses to praise Him.

As we yielded all areas of our lives to God, blessings rained down on us. Hardly a day went by that we didn't feel a shower of these mini-miracles.

Friends and relatives were equally elated and confused by the things we were sharing with them. By now, we were getting quite bold in our witnessing. We would have had a hard time stifling the urge to tell everyone about the Guest in our home.

I looked for every possible source of Christian growth. I continued with the Bible-study group every Tuesday. Those lovely ladies provided sympathetic strength and encouragement as I continued in the role of a single parent.

As we studied the Bible, it was fascinating to find how relevant it was to my life that day! It was also more refreshing than the dire news in the daily paper. It was up-to-date in prophetic news too.

I thought my encounter with God was most unique, until I was introduced to the local Christian Women's Club. Here was a friendly and hospitable group of women. They invited ladies to come from the entire area. Their homes were open every month for Bible studies and prayer coffees. This wasn't the usual type of women's club where the purpose might be philanthropic and the members carefully selected for their social prestige. The purpose of the Christian Women's Clubs was to introduce women to Jesus Christ so their lives could be revitalized. I took a minor job on the board.

In May 1972 an evangelist came to the Parma Heights church to conduct a "Christian Life and Witness" course. It was part of the preliminary work before the Billy Graham Crusade to be held in Cleveland in July 1972. This course was just what we needed to gain more knowledge about our new life-style. We had lived in the historical remembrance of Jesus Christ. Now we needed guidance in living in the *fellowship* of Jesus.

Later, the crusade was a mighty tool in bringing the rest of the children to the Lord. We were able to attend nearly every night because of Christian friends who were assigned as counselors or ushers.

Two children answered the invitation to come forward and receive Christ during the crusade. I see the value of this overt act. In deliberately walking forward to the altar, one decides to turn his back on the world, regardless of peer pressure, and say, "Lord, I choose You."

In spite of spiritual victories, the summer of 1972 had not been easy for me. Tom and David had gone to live in Florida. Undoubtedly, they hoped distance would ease their unhappiness. My husband dropped in for brief visits on the weekends. Occasionally he would take the children out to eat or invite them to spend a weekend with him in his apartment.

Our house was very lonely with three important male members now absent.

Our time of family prayer had a rich meaning for all of us. It was a powerful tool of strength every time we exercised it. We were open and unashamed to ask God for the help we needed to get through the day. We recognized Him as our source of strength.

One day in September 1972, I asked the children to gather around me for prayer before they left for their first day of school. It was beautiful to see those nine heads bowed for prayer. There were no doubters or scoffers in that group.

I asked God to be very near each one of them. Some were apprehensive about going to new buildings or meeting new teachers. I closed, simply asking God to bless our day. God was listening.

We were all especially lonely for David. He had been the big brother whom we could all call on for help. He understood Steven's need to ride a dirt bike in the wheat field or have a hamburger before bedtime. Steve had followed him wherever he went. I couldn't take

David's place for Steve, and I shared Steve's loneliness for David.

Everyone of us prayed that God would speak to David's heart so that he would decide to come home to us. We prayed, and we expected to get an answer. Perhaps that is one requirement to successful prayer. Pray and *expect* to get results! We knew that David owned a small motorcycle, so every time we heard a bike, we'd dash to the window.

The house seemed unnaturally quiet once the children were gone to school. All the outside noises were louder, and the drone of a motorcycle seemed very close. I looked out the window. Sure enough, my David was climbing off the seat! He apologized for the fuzzy beard that tickled through my kisses. We just stood in the driveway for the longest time laughing and crying with joy. Eventually, I remembered to offer him some lunch.

David had a story to tell us. At a crossroad in Georgia, a woman had neglected to stop for a stop sign. It was raining hard, and both her car and David's bike slid on the wet pavement. David's leg was caught behind her front bumper. As the vehicles came to a stop, the bumper pulled loose, releasing David's leg. A group of men ran over from a nearby filling station. All of them were amazed that David still had a leg. A week before, three men had been killed at that same intersection.

I was glad we had prayed for our needs that morning. A sober-faced David confided that he had stopped every hundred miles under the nearest tree to thank God for safety. He remained with us for the balance of the school year.

By December 3, 1972, six of us were ready for baptism. Edith and her husband filled their ranch-style house for a reception in our honor. We had a memorable party time after the services in church. There were singing, games, and delicious food.

Edith and Paul were just two of the beautiful Christians who had encouraged us and helped us learn the more abundant way to live.

I couldn't help but observe that with all the fun of the evening, there wasn't a single cocktail or glass of beer in the room. No one was embarrassed or sick the next day. The living water of Jesus Christ provided all we needed for refreshment.

6

When I became a Christian, one of the verses my eager ears tuned in was John 10:10. The second half of the verse promises abundant life. What did that mean to me? It didn't take me long to realize that the abundant life did not mean things, nor did it mean even a lack of problems. I was experiencing a never ending series of tests and trials. The answer finally dawned on me. Now that I was a child of God, I could claim all God's promises to see me through the problems. In 1 Corinthians 1:7 I read a beautiful truth: "Now you have every grace and blessing; every spiritual gift and power for doing his will are yours during this time of waiting for the return of our Lord Jesus Christ" (TLB). The Bible does not promise us a trouble-free life, rather it promises that the grace of God will see us through each problem as we turn it over to God. By the gift of faith, we can believe and receive the help we need. Our strength may not be sufficient, but God's is!

The Bible says our trials and troubles are meant to strengthen and improve us. I needed much improvement. I needed all the fruit of the Spirit. I freely admitted lacking patience, wisdom, love for others, and much more.

God began His mighty work in me. The circumstances in my life did not change, but my attitude toward them changed. Most noticeable was my new attitude toward people. I had been taught to be nice to others. I had acquired the usual set of manners and proper behavior. The problem was I didn't have any deep feeling for people. Mine was a superficial sorrow for their grief. I could walk away feeling glad that the problem was theirs, not mine. Without Christ, we are all extremely selfish. Even nice people think of themselves first.

I was always very selective when I chose a new friend. The people that didn't measure up to my standards were politely ignored. In Christian fellowship, people genuinely care for each other. It must be the Spirit of God that makes it possible!

Truly, that is what Jesus meant when He said we are to love our neighbors as ourselves. None of us can cultivate such a life-style without the grace of God.

We had attended one church for seven years, and we had barely known seven people! Everyone had been so busy doing his own thing. It had been a nuisance to have that collection plate passed for missions. Let those who have an overabundance do the helping. We had a family of our own to take care of. Surely, God understood that. I wonder now where our children would have learned to love and share if we had set such a limited example of charity for them. It never occurred to me to worry about that.

During my high school years, I had deliberately snubbed a man at work. I considered him too coarse and earthy an individual. I sat next to his sister in school, and she told me she had a glass of wine for breakfast. I gasped in shock. I didn't have the maturity required to realize other people have other life-styles, or in this case, a very inadequate income. Something or someone directed the members of this family to a higher goal. I was chagrined to observe this man years

51

later. He was totally devoted to his wife and children. Lord, forgive my intolerance.

Being the mother of eleven children, I obviously liked children—but who needs number twelve? I had done my share of diapers. I had cleaned up my share of messes. Now I felt ready to admire all little ones from a distance. Then God began to deal with me over such inadequate love.

News reached me that a neighboring family was in great need. The father of six small children had had a nervous breakdown. His pregnant wife was keeping bread on the table by doing substitute teaching. Her biggest problem was finding a baby-sitter for her two-year-old daughter. My own three-year-old was extremely lonely since her next sister had gone off to a full day of school. Like the other children, Barbie felt the upheaval of the home. She knew Daddy and her two big brothers were no longer living at home. She had begun to throw tantrums and whine. Her behavioral problems didn't do much for my mental health. An idea took form. Could it be that I would actually benefit by helping my neighbor? The Bible clearly told me to give that I might receive!

Little Cathy arrived every morning. The mother understood that if for some reason the two little girls didn't get along, the whole plan would have to be scrapped. But as soon as the initial shyness wore off, Cathy and Barbie were the greatest of friends. They shared toys, clothes, and peanut butter sandwiches as if it were a glorious adventure. It proved to be a happy arrangement for both families.

My neighbors were observing me now that I talked about God. Did they see my actions change for the better? I felt like I was living in a fish bowl, yet if I preached the value of a Christ-centered life, I would need to set a good example. In my busy life, I didn't have time to scheme or set the stage for the goodness to shine through. *If* they saw Christ in me, it would have to be from God.

I had had a problem with a little two-year-old son of a good friend in the neighborhood. Like all little boys, Jimmy was full of life. I had no trouble remembering the antics of my own five sons, but I had a hard time tolerating ten sticky fingers in a stranger. When he wasn't pulling the dog's hair, he found another avenue of mischief. While we women tried to visit, he could be a nuisance, demanding constant attention from his doting mother. When Jean brought him over to the house, I would catch my breath and hope for the best while I stashed all the breakables in a safe place. Fortunately, our home had become quite child-proof over the years.

I began to be convicted. Another neighbor took Jimmy in stride, seemingly even loving the boy more than the knicknacks she had collected over the years. Surely, God did not approve of the deep resentment I was trying to cover up. I began to pray that I might feel love for Jimmy—more than just a tolerance.

On the next visit, I determined to put feet to my prayers. I dropped to my knees in front of the bewildered boy. I took his hands in my hands and said, "Jimmy, I love you very much." In an instant, he flew into my arms and planted a juicy kiss on my cheek. "I love you so much *too!*" From that moment on, Jimmy ceased to be as obnoxious as an ant climbing up the wall. He was a little boy that I could love through Christ. The friendship between his mother and me grew too.

I was willing to change every area of my life except my marital status. It seemed to me that God, who had rescued me from death, could surely rescue a dead marriage too. I continued to pray for such a miracle.

My husband resisted all my pleadings for a reconciliation.

"What would you do if I died?" I knew if he had died first, I would have crawled into the grave with his body. There was no possibility I would have survived his death. I was totally committed to being his wife for the length of my life.

When I pleaded with him for help to rear the nine minor children, he reminded me that I had managed very well while he was gone on long business trips. It was true that most of that type of responsibility had fallen on my shoulders during his absences, but we had always been confident of his return on the weekend.

I was also concerned for my husband's life. He admitted that the apartment was a very lonely place to live. He missed the children, but not enough to come back to our home.

"What have I done? How can I change so you will love me again?"

His staid appearance failed to reveal any sign of compassion for me. "You haven't done anything. We simply grew apart."

That answer was small consolation, because if I had been guilty of something, there would have been a possibility of reform. His answer made it all a dead issue. He wanted to go on with plans for a life apart from me.

Finally, on the advice of my doctor and the pastor, I signed a settlement agreement in February 1973.

Two neighbors came into court with me to testify that I was a proper parent to raise all the minor children. It struck me as being preposterous for the wisest of judges to delegate such a huge responsibility to one person. God, in His wisdom, had given every child *two* parents. Perhaps the learned judge had private reservations of his own. I felt like someone had just told me to manage General Motors or any such sizable venture. Surely God would have to be my partner, and His Word assured me of His loving protection and guidance in our lives.

I dreaded the day of the next court appearance. My attorney tried to reassure me of the "simple" procedure, but I could foresee it only as a real ordeal. I had seen some of the gruesome telecasts of the program "Divorce Court." The two parties would scream insults and accusations at each other in the cold, impersonal atmosphere of a courtroom. The thought of personally living through such turmoil was almost unbearable. I knew I would never make it without God's help. As early as possible, I began a daily routine of prayer for strength just for those terrible moments I had to face in court.

Five minutes before I left for the courthouse, a dear Christian friend called to assure me of the prayers of my many new friends. He told me to take on the whole armor of God during this painful experience. Then we praised God because the Bible promises, "All things work together for good to them that love God, to them who are the called according to his purpose" (Romans 8:28).

It was God's plan for me. While it wasn't what I would have chosen, I was sure of God's peace in this situation.

The courtrooms were busy with lawyers and their clients. We took a seat on one of the long benches to wait. Watching the people was very interesting. Some faces were lined with deep care and anxiety. I noticed the predominance of teenage girls with very small babies in their arms. It was horrifying to realize that the idea of divorce was conceived as early as the infant lying in their arms. I was overwhelmed with compassion for those girls who had had to become adults too soon. I completely forgot my own circumstances and unhappiness.

When it was my turn, there were brief questions by both attorneys, and then the legal papers were handed to the judge, who sat at the head of the table. The session was very brief, just as my attorney had promised. He had been reluctant to act in a case where such a large number of children were involved. I know he hoped my husband would reconsider his actions during the past months. He was perspiring with concern after the meeting. Why do such things happen to two nice people? Who knows the answer to that?

A stone had once come out of my dainty wedding ring. I hadn't taken that wedding ring off for nineteen years through all the hours of childbirth and the lighter moments. The jeweler asked me to remove the ring so he could examine the setting.

"Do I have to take the ring off?"

He smiled at my hesitation. Perhaps I was being silly to be so sentimental about a ring, but it was a very precious symbol to me. Actually, the ring was so bent and worn, it needed to be replaced. Now it seemed to be God's plan that I give up my "idol."

We had a lovely photo album made of our wedding pictures. All the special moments of the ceremony were thus recorded. Now, the photos have curled up, and the binding has disintegrated.

The church where we were married has been torn down and replaced. The new modern structure bears no resemblance to the little country church where we said our vows.

My husband remarried in the summer of 1973. He lives far away, and his visits are infrequent.

Praise the Lord anyway!

The time has finally come when I recognize that God

can use a tragedy. Satan engineered the evil plans, but God used the circumstances to bring my family close to Him for His glory and honor.

Like the Pharisee, I had stood before God. I had been so proud of *my* perfect husband, *my* beautiful children, and *my* talent in the home. Wasn't God pleased with my successful living?

And God's Word said, "All our righteousnesses are as filthy rags" (Isaiah 64:6). I was convicted of worshiping my husband instead of God. The Lord taught me to understand the pain of rejection He felt when I didn't recognize His gift of love to me on the cross at Calvary.

Drastic, yes! Who can question the wisdom of God? Who can understand His plans? The prophet Hosea was permitted to marry a prostitute so he would understand the fickleness of the nation Israel.

I must only consider the great mercy of God. He forgave my sins. He didn't let me die, even though I pleaded for an end of it all. Instead, He gave me the divine command to live in the fellowship of His Son, Jesus Christ.

7

I had fought the divorce for over two years. Marriage had been a total commitment for me. As a child I had been the product of a broken marriage. My parents had separated when I was only four months old. My father was someone I thought about, but I have never seen him except in a snapshot.

As a schoolgirl I envied the classmates that could talk about their fathers. I envied the girls that could talk about an older brother or sister, but especially a big brother. I thought that to have a dad or a big brother must be the neatest thing in the world to anyone.

Early in my teenage years, I had resolved not to date any boy I considered a questionable risk as stable, secure husband-material. I wanted a husband so honorable and trustworthy that I would never wonder whether he was faithful to me. Infidelity was unthinkable, because my children were going to have the most secure and happy homelife I could give them, or I would stay single. Those were strong sentiments I had held for all the years I dated in high school and college.

Whenever my husband and I had sat in the audience to witness our children in a choir or some other public performance, I had thought about how fortunate the children were to have two parents sitting there. My mother had come to Girl Scout court of awards and the usual potluck dinners, but it was hard for her. She had been the single parent who had had to provide for all my needs. I was very aware of her struggle to support us and meet the basic needs of a growing child while attempting to find a satisfying life-style for herself.

When my husband would argue his case for a divorce—"What's wrong with divorce? Everyone is doing it!"—I could only groan with despair deep down in my spirit. He didn't know the same lonely childhood I did. He was being swayed by the liberals of today. I believed that no problem in a marriage is too big to be solved if both people try to find a solution that is not entirely selfish. I had to swallow a bitter pill of disappointment when I was forced to realize that one partner cannot keep a marriage together without the cooperation of the other. I gave in, against my better judgment.

When I faced the reality of the divorce, I felt a new sense of personal freedom. I was released from the restrictions that marriage had placed on me. My life was not wrapped up in plans to make life easier or more pleasant for my husband. I was now free, if you could call a woman with nine minor children free in any sense of the word.

The final divorce papers came in the mail early in April 1973. It was difficult to shake the sadness, but there were suddenly some compensations to cheer me and encourage me.

Most families have to live where the father is employed. With the divorce final, I was free to build a new life for myself and the children. I felt an urgency to try my wings at such a prospect.

I had lost my identity during all those years when I

59

was confined to the house with eleven children and thirteen rooms of housework. When I heard my husband call me "Gloria," it had a most unfamiliar ring to it. There was so little of Gloria. She had lived such a closely confined life, almost like a hothouse plant, protected from the wind of adversity by the love of a conciliatory mate.

I would *find* Gloria! I also needed to take an inventory and evaluate what was left to build on.

God gives everyone a measure of talent. What were my talents, besides a good pie crust or a straight seam?

Obviously, I couldn't go on producing prize-winning children. I didn't like the picture of a mother spending the rest of her life clinging to her children for security. They must be free to grow and then leave.

My husband suggested I look forward to the grandchildren. Well, thank you, but what about the years in between?

After much thought and prayer, I decided to enjoy a vacation suggested by my eldest son. Tom lived in Florida. Every winter I had seen my neighbors leave for the sunny, warm climate while we got the plow and snow shovels ready for work. They brought me glowing tales of the warmth and the beautiful flowers. I wanted to see for myself.

Earlier I mentioned a terrible fear of flying. When God gave me the divine command to live, He graciously took away many of the fears and anxieties that I had lived with most of my life. I had been able to fly back to Wisconsin for a visit, and I regarded the flight as one of the most exhilarating experiences I had ever enjoyed. I was looking forward to another flight to Florida with great eagerness.

Tom's letters encouraged us to consider moving to a

warm climate. David had already decided he was through with snow and ice. He wasn't willing to spend any more winters in Ohio.

"Lord, what is Your will for this family?" Family devotions became a time for serious searching and discussion with the Lord. The children were generous in their encouragement.

The older children understood that we could not afford to keep the big house. The driveway needed expensive repairs. The beautiful pool had provided much enjoyment, but now it was a financial liability. In a short time, the repairs and upkeep on the property would bankrupt me. According to the terms of the settlement, I would have trouble even making the mortgage payments.

Another big factor was my husband's announcement that he intended to remarry in a few months. He was in the process of buying a new home just four miles away.

The thought of sharing my children and my husband with wife number two was more than I could bear. The Bible said that Jesus died for me and this other woman too. Jesus loved her, and I must forgive her. Could I blame her for falling in love with a "perfect" man? How could she resist his charm, kindness, and consideration?

I counted on God to heal the pain and turmoil her presence produced. Rebellion against God's command to forgive would have a paralyzing effect on my spiritual growth. I couldn't change by myself. God would have to help me, and for the moment, all I had to offer was a willingness to change.

Satan was always at work. I had waves of depression threaten me whenever her name was mentioned. Clearly, I wasn't strong enough to live four miles from this new wife.

I proceeded with plans to visit Tom in Daytona Beach, Florida. In Daytona, my prayers were very earnest and serious. I recognized how much was at stake.

I dropped to my knees that very first morning. My nervous breakdown had left me with little strength to make a decision of that magnitude, and I was aware of that. I felt as unsteady as a new colt not yet air-dried. God would have to hold me up with His strength. He alone could keep me from making costly blunders.

Early in our marriage, my husband and I had been misled by a smooth salesman. We had purchased a lot, only to learn after making payments for a year, that the county was not issuing any more sewer and water permits for that parcel of land. Eventually, we sold our piece to a speculator who could afford to keep the land until conditions changed. It was a lesson to us.

I went down to the lobby of the Florida hotel. The first step was to buy a newspaper and scan the real estate ads. At the very top of the list was an ad that read "Five bedroom ranch—just $23,000." Surely that couldn't be much of a house! It seemed to be a ridiculously low price, but on the other hand, I didn't know the property values in this area. Perhaps houses sold for less than they would in Ohio. We had also discussed the fact that we would have to settle for a lower standard of living, housing included, than we had been accustomed to in the preceding ten years.

I phoned the real estate office. An obliging young man arranged for a tour of the property in the next hour.

Over and over I prayed, *God, give me wisdom. Don't let me be swayed by a fast-talking salesman.*

The salesman was not high pressure at all! In fact, I was won over by his calm, quiet charm. He understood that I would have to sell the big house in Ohio before I could buy any house in Florida.

A tour of the house and the yard full of graceful palm trees left me filled with enthusiasm. I was sure this was the house for us, but just to make sure, I asked to see the house one more time when Tom could join me. Tom was the one who would give me a hint to the other children's reaction. He had always been the gauge for all the family activities. If I tried a new recipe, Tom tasted it first. The other children watched his reaction. If he made a face, I could be fairly sure that no one else would eat it either. It was maddening.

Tom was still the big brother. I watched as he walked through the house. He asked the real estate salesman some questions about the possible inadequacy of the heating system. I barely heard his comment. Surely that would be insignificant.

Even the area where the house was located seemed to suit us perfectly. We were only two blocks from a large shopping center. I could envision jobs for the children there after school and during the summer. I wouldn't need a car for shopping with the stores so conveniently located. We wouldn't need expensive winter clothing. I was just ecstatic over my discovery!

We went back to the office to sign a purchase agreement. The purchase of this house was contingent on the sale of the house in Ohio.

With the big problem behind me, I thoroughly enjoyed the next three days of my brief vacation in Florida. It was pure delight to breathe in the fresh salt air. No putrid smell of steel mills down here.

Tom gave me all his time over the weekend. He did his very best to give me a memorable time, and I was grateful. The last few months of winter had been so hectic and traumatic, I was gasping for a breath of refreshment.

Tom stopped to pick up an order of hamburgers or fried chicken, and then we were off to enjoy Marineland or a ride in the glass-bottomed boat at Silver Springs. He was anxious for me to appreciate the beauties of Daytona Beach. We drove around in the Holly Hill area. He pointed out the river where private boats were docked. At Christmas the river comes alive when Christmas trees are floated downstream. Tom's enthusiasm was contagious, and I couldn't wait to share it with the family.

Once back in Ohio, I told our plans to the children, and to relatives and friends. All the relatives seemed dubious that this move was the wisest one for us to make. Those in Wisconsin felt I should return to that state. They all offered to help me with the job of parenthood. The Christian friends in Ohio seemed concerned that I had the wrong motive for wanting to leave Ohio. They could understand the financial reasons. It was my stubborn refusal to give the new arrangement a try until our lives were more stabilized. I had a mental block. I would not be a baby-sitter for my husband during the week and then on weekends let him decide which of the children he and his new wife would entertain while I stayed home with the balance. It was just too one-sided an arrangement to suit me. What if she won my children, as she had my husband? It was cruel to be buffetted by these winds of adversity. I had to protect myself from any more pain, and I would do it by moving far away.

Of course, my husband learned about my plans to leave Ohio. He was not won over when the children assured him they wanted to live in Florida as much as their mother did.

My ex-husband reacted in the only possible way. He wanted the court to decide if I should move the children out of Ohio.

I was terribly upset, not for myself, but now the children would be subjected to a traumatic court appearance. They would be forced to select the parent they preferred. That seemed to me to be the one thing we had both tried to avoid from the beginning of the conflict.

In the meantime, the children and I began a general sorting and cleaning of the accumulation of the past ten years. Surely, the Lord would work out the problem without further pain. I prayed with real confidence, trusting that the answer, whatever it might be, would be God's will.

My next step was a visit to the newspaper office. I couldn't keep the big house. There wasn't any possible way we could afford it.

A middle-aged woman sat at the desk in the office. She appeared so tired and unresponsive that I finally helped her compose the ad myself. *Thirteen-room house on a three-acre lot. 16 x 40 in-the-ground pool. Three-car garage and out buildings.*

The woman looked up at me and asked, "Why would you want to sell such a beautiful property?" By her expression, I could feel a genuine concern, not just female inquisitiveness.

I gave her a brief explanation, but I hastened to tell her that God was real in our lives. I was sure He had a new house for us that suited us better. Her eyes turned very sad, and she confided that she wished she could find God. She had been looking for Him a long time. We were the only two people in the small room. It was easy to have the intimate atmosphere where two hearts could speak to God, and when I left the lady, she was smiling with the new hope that had been born in her heart.

She was a substitute worker, just in the office that one afternoon of the week. Once more, I felt God was directing my path. I had been obedient to His directions; He would not forsake me.

8

On May 26, 1973, I was aware that my two sons were planning some big adventure. It was a long holiday weekend for David from his job, and Steven would have a vacation from school.

The boys were reluctant to tell me that they planned a motorcycle trip to Virginia. David thought Steve would enjoy a trip to the beautiful Shenandoah Valley region. Our eldest son, Tom, had completed high school at Massannutten Military Academy in Woodstock, Virginia.

The boys tried to reassure me of their safety by giving me full details of their trip. They planned to stay on the safer back roads to avoid the heavy holiday traffic. That didn't put down my maternal apprehension.

The boys were restless now that winter was over. I knew how boring the long weekend could be. It was the sight of Steven's small body on the back of the bike that really upset me. What amount of protection did that small sissy bar afford to the passenger? No, I couldn't agree to this trip. David scoffed at my fears. He reminded me that he had driven 10,000 miles without getting hurt.

Clearly, it was no use to argue. They roared out of the yard. I watched in apprehension until the sound of the motor died in the distance.

It was Margaret's tenth birthday. She elected to go to the Parmatown shopping center for lunch at Higbee's dining balcony. Afterward, we shopped for a few gifts. It would have been a very pleasant day, if only I could have forgotten my anxiety over the two boys on the motorcycle trip.

The boys would often coax me to ride behind them on their bikes, but that speed without the protection of an enclosure was too dangerous for me to enjoy. I prayed that the weekend would go fast.

After dinner in the evening, the children joined me for family devotions. The little ones had their usual list of petitions and prayers for all the sick people. I was anxious to pray for David and Steven.

Supper had been later than usual, and it was nearly seven by the time we finished our prayers. Our worship time ended abruptly when the telephone rang. Ann jumped to answer it. Her face froze with concern. Then, she burst into tears. I was on my feet in a moment to take the telephone from her. A soft-voiced nurse was calling me from the Winchester Memorial Hospital in Virginia.

She was telling me that my two sons had just been admitted to the hospital. Her voice was strained as she broke the dire news. David had two broken legs, and Steven was in intensive care with severe brain damage. He had less than a 50-50 chance of survival. I was having real trouble comprehending the enormity of this tragic news. I didn't panic.

I felt my ex-husband was probably working at the new house he had just purchased. I made a very brief phone call to him, and we agreed to rush to our sons in the hospital.

Children were crying all around me. The older girls went off to pack a suitcase for me. Others started clearing the supper table. Karen and Paul had left us earlier to attend a church youth meeting. Someone called them. Mary called the leader of the Bible-study group. These ladies would give us prayerful support through the ordeal.

Ann handed me a packed suitcase as her father drove into the yard. I grabbed most of a box of tissues as we literally ran out of the door.

Filling stations had begun to limit the sale of gasoline to ten gallons per customer, but under the circumstances, the attendant agreed to fill our tank.

We sped off in the dark toward the Pennsylvania turnpike. The man sitting next to me was crying so hard, I wondered how he could see to drive. Over and over he would repeat, "Let's just trust God." Just for the time being, I felt I should trust God to get us over the wet mountain roads. Periodically, he would reach over to take my hand. That seemed strange after the events of the past three years.

We clasped hands briefly at times, but I urged him to hold fast to the steering wheel. I got a degree of solace out of gripping the shoulder strap with all my might. I wondered if I might pull it loose!

Romans 8:28 raced through by brain again: *All things work together for good to them that love God, to them who are the called according to his purpose.* God was allowing this tragedy. Was it another test for me? Was it a test for the father of these boys? God had proved Himself faithful. I could trust Him now.

As my ex-husband sobbed and wiped his eyes, I watched the road. The weather was getting worse by the mile. Light rain and patches of fog grew more frequent as we raced around the mountains. The heavy trucks seemed menacingly close to the small compact car as we drove past them in the left lane.

Finally, we were off the turnpike and speeding toward Winchester. We had often driven Tom back to Woodstock, twenty miles from Winchester.

The fog had become denser. The two-lane road was increasingly dangerous, and we began the last few miles of the trip crawling along just below fifteen miles an hour. We were both frantic to get to the hospital, but the situation was nearly impossible. The strain was terrible! I prayed out loud, "God, send us some help!"

In just a matter of seconds, a city vehicle passed us with a high-beam light that sliced through the thick fog. We had no trouble following the truck to the city limits. At that point we noticed a police car parked on the other side of the street. My ex-husband rolled down the window to call to the policeman in the car. "Where is the hospital?" The obliging policeman called back, "Follow me," and he led us directly to the hospital parking lot. As we ran to the emergency entrance, we saw the dim figure of a man in the doorway. He called out to us, "Are you the Hursts?" It was Steven's doctor.

How can anyone doubt God's hand in the events of the evening? We had made the trip in record time, in spite of the fog and rain. Then a city vehicle, a policeman, and now the doctor were all positioned exactly where we would need them.

We were led down a flight of stairs to see Steven. Our son lay directly in front of the nurse's desk. He had been spared facial injuries. His eyes were slightly open, and he was breathing very rapidly. The monitor above his head gave off a rapid beep-beep sound. Only a young, strong heart could endure such pressure and trauma. The doctor explained that the brain was damaged on the right side. Since there was no room for swelling in the skull, Steven's blood pressure was soaring.

70

Suddenly, my legs began to buckle. My husband explained to the doctor that I had had a nervous breakdown. I hadn't taken any pills as a regular routine for so long, I didn't think to pack any. The doctor gave me some Valium.

We were confident that Steven was getting the best possible care, so we made our way up to David's room. Poor David! Not only had he gone through the terrible trauma of the accident, but now he was full of anxiety for his brother. We did our best to calm him and tell him that everything was fine.

David began to explain how he and Steve had come through the fog in search of a motel for the night. As they slowed down to turn into the driveway, a car hit them from the rear. Steve's helmet stuck on the sissy bar when his head was thrown back on impact. Minus the protective headgear, he flew through the air with a piercing scream of pain and fright.

David was able to stay on the bike a few seconds more, and he landed in the gravel on his knees and then his head. His helmet was pockmarked from the impact of the stones, but he was spared a head injury similar to Steve's. We were relieved to see that David's legs were not broken as first reported. His legs had felt numb because of the sudden shock, and they had been doubled up under his body. The ambulance attendants had assumed from that awkward position that the legs were broken.

David said the ambulance had arrived minutes after the accident. Steven was moved first because of the severity of his injuries. David had some bruises on his hands and shoulder. His T-shirt and jacket were shredded, but as in Georgia, God had spared him serious injury.

Although I felt calm inside, my legs began to react. I had trouble walking. My husband half carried me into the hotel. Every nerve was responding to the crisis, and I began to shake uncontrollably. A glance at my husband's stricken features told me he should have been given some medication too. His tears continued through the night, and I doubt he slept much.

After an early breakfast, we hurried back to the hospital. David was out of bed and demanding to see Steven. He was a bit shaky, but his doctor agreed David could go in a wheelchair to see Steve. We realized that David needed to see for himself that Steven was still alive. Steve's condition hadn't changed overnight. The nurses urged us to call Steve by name and to talk to him on the mere chance that he could hear us without being able to respond. He was in a deep coma, but he would groan and toss on the bed. The signs of life encouraged us, but the doctor said they were common and meaningless.

I was thankful that God had spared Steven's face and limbs. I had especially prayed that his eyes would be intact as we drove through the night. Any girl would have been happy to have those blue eyes and long lashes. We were told that Steve had severe abrasions on his back, and there was a burn on his neck where the helmet strap resisted the force. He could have been seriously scarred, and it was wonderful to believe that God had heard us.

David was sent back to bed, and we could visit Steven's bedside every hour for ten minutes. The balance of the time we stayed with David. He needed to be reassured and loved.

In the evening, we located a rooming house just two blocks from the hospital. I planned to stay in Winchester the next week. David and my ex-husband had to return to their jobs.

My aunt had been visiting us in Cleveland at the

time of the accident. She agreed to stay on awhile longer if I needed to stay with Steven in Virginia.

My ex-husband agreed to stop at the house every night to help her with the other children. We would exchange nightly telephone calls so he could know the doctor's reports on Steven's condition. Our differences had all dissolved for the time being. We were able to communicate again after years of dissension. It seemed a miracle! Was this the purpose for the accident? It had certainly produced a time when we would not be selfishly concerned for ourselves. We shared instead a mutual concern for our sons.

There was further evidence of a new concern for me in his attitude. The night of the accident he relented in his determination to fight our move to Florida. If we were determined to live away from him, he would have his attorney withdraw the legal action against me.

Thank You, Lord.

The days in Virginia went by one by one. I had time to think as I walked the distance from the hospital back to the rooming house. Was it possible that this tragedy would return a husband and father to us? Would my husband give up *his* plan to live away from us? He was such a sensitive and proud man. Would it be too difficult for him to retrace his steps and come back to us? Would he realize how fortunate he was to have so much love waiting for him after this amount of time?

The nearness of God sustained me with an unbelievable peace in all matters. God was in complete control of my life and Steven's.

At Easter, Steven had appeared before the board of deacons as a candidate for water baptism and church membership. Part of my young son's testimony was a request to spend the rest of his life walking with God.

Now, he was totally in God's care. He was a child of the King.

On Tuesday, as I stood at Steven's bedside, I could see that he was having a low period in his struggle between life and death. He was very flushed, and the urgency of the noisy monitor was at a very high pitch. I felt personally tested. Could I give up my son? Had my faith grown sufficiently to pass this test? Steve was a sweet little boy that had rarely left my side. He was beside me every morning while I prepared the variety of cold lunches for the school kids. This one took ham; this one insisted on a bologna sandwich without mayonnaise. Steve was the memory bank, so each one got his own preference. Steven was *my* boy.

I had had such heartbreaking pain for over three years. Would God require me to suffer another loss?

God promises, "My grace is sufficient for thee: for my strength is made perfect in weakness" (2 Corinthians 12:9). I freely admitted to being one of God's weakest children. I had no recourse except to trust in the tender mercy of my heavenly Father.

On Wednesday morning, Steven's doctor took a few minutes to sit in the hall with me. He confirmed my suspicions about Steven's condition on the previous day. In fact, Steve had not fully recovered, and suction was necessary to drain the fluid that was collecting in his chest. The doctors were considering performing a tracheotomy to prevent Steve from dying of pneumonia. He wouldn't feel the surgery, but as his mother, I would! It was another test for me. But the tracheotomy was never performed.

I had to ask the doctor if Steve would recover sufficiently to live a normal life. Without hesitation, he replied that Steve would recover but I shouldn't expect any change in his condition for at least two weeks.

While I ate breakfast the next morning, my peace was shaken. The community was small enough for townspeople to recognize strangers. The man sitting next to me had asked to have the salt passed. It was not long before he was telling me his son had been hospitalized with severe brain damage a year before.

The young man had been in a coma for three months. I began to wonder if the doctor was merely trying to spare me further worry when he predicted that my son would not regain consciousness for two weeks. Might it be in fact more than two months?

The most distressing part of my vigil at Steven's bedside was not the sight of my own son. The bed next to his held a poor girl who had been severely injured in a car accident that same fateful night. She had hit a row of guard posts, and one of them had come inside the car, and literally ripped off her leg. Her nose was broken, and they had had to remove her appendix while they explored for internal injuries.

How thankful I was for the whole body of my son! He looked as if he were in a deep sleep.

I spent my ten-minute visits with Steve, leaning over his bed. I would tell him I loved him and reassure him of my presence.

I tried to stand with my back to the elevated stump of that leg in the next bed. Poor girl.

My telephone bill mounted as I called home to Ohio. My family and concerned friends were anxious for news. The minister also was concerned for all of us. He said his phone was ringing day and night as the people of the church wanted to hear the latest reports. "You have almost caused a revival!" he told me. God's people feel genuine compassion. Pain that touches one member of the Body of Christ affects all the other members.

My family was overfed by the generous church people. A full course dinner was delivered every night while I stayed in Virginia. The people were quite generous. Because my family was so large, two or three families joined together to provide the meal. The refrigerator groaned with leftovers.

There were constant prayers offered for all of us. I could feel the strength of those prayers for myself and at Steven's bedside.

I visited Steven twice in the morning, and three times in the afternoon, then once more in the evening after my seven-o'clock telephone call to Ohio. There was never any noticeable change in Steve's condition.

I had my Bible but no other reading material. As I wandered around the quaint and interesting streets of Winchester, I stumbled across a Christian bookstore, The Mustard Seed. It was hidden down a flight of stairs. There were two rooms of Christian books. What a delight!

During my second visit, I became acquainted with the young clerk. We began sharing the marvelous experiences of God in our lives. She had been delivered from drugs and a sordid life that would have eventually destroyed her. Jesus had rescued her as He had me, so we had a mutual bond even though we were total strangers.

One of the books I purchased was *God's Smuggler.* As I sat in the lobby of the hospital, I found myself royally entertained by the activities of Brother Andrew. Here was a simple man hard at work for the kingdom of God, despite the dangers of detection.

Steven's father joined me again on the next weekend. There was still no change in Steve's condition. He would moan and toss on the bed, sometimes kicking his feet violently. They had to be encased in booties similar to those I had tried to keep on his feet when he was an infant.

After the weekend, it was decided that I would return to Ohio for a week with the other children. I would call the doctor for frequent reports on Steve's condition.

While I was in Virginia, people had been inquiring about the sale of the house. Karen had given one couple the grand tour, and they were ready to sign a purchase agreement. I had decided I must go through with the sale. The marriage was over, and with God's help, we would build a new life. I would notify the real estate people that we could go ahead with the purchase of the house in Florida.

The next weekend we took Peter and Paul back to Virginia with us. They were anxious to check on their brother's condition.

We were surprised when we got to the hospital and learned that Steven had been taken out of the intensive care unit. He had a bed right in front of a big window in the pediatric ward. The nurses' desk was right on the other side of the window. They were able to watch his moment-by-moment progress. He had begun to regain consciousness on Friday.

The doctor teased, "Steve is making too much fuss for the ICU, that is a place for *sick* people." Obviously, everyone was very pleased to see a young boy return to life. What a miracle! It had not taken two weeks for Steven to wake up; he had done it in just ten days!

Because the injury was to the right side of the brain, Steven had lost the use of his left side. He was quite upset when he discovered that he couldn't walk. Once awake, he wanted to stand up and leave the hospital. He motioned for me to bend down so he could whisper in my ear.

77

"Pray for me, Mom, I can't walk."

He did not know about the thousands of prayers that had been offered up for him since the accident.

The nurses put a bell on the table near enough for him to reach. It was a delight to see him reach over and tap it with one finger.

Over the weekend we could see his memory gradually return. He recognized his brothers, and most of the familiar incidents returned to his mind. The accident was mercifully blotted from his memory for almost the extent of his hospital stay.

He had some difficulty with speech. He would scratch the sheet when he wanted his back scratched. The abrasions were healing, but the medication never seemed to relieve the terrible itching. Steve would get very impatient with me for avoiding the sorest areas.

It made me cringe to see his great difficulties, and yet, his progress was astounding all of us.

Steve's father drew a tick-tack-toe game on his notebook. Steven had no trouble making his mark and trying to win the game. His left side remained lifeless, so eventually, we put his wristwatch on his right arm.

Steve made such remarkable progress that the doctor agreed I could charter a plane to fly Steven back to a Cleveland hospital. I was anxious to get back to the other children.

My ex-husband and I went to the First Baptist Church of Winchester every Sunday that we were in the city. The people of the church were very friendly, and the pastor called on Steve whenever he got to the hospital.

This was to be our last Sunday in Winchester. I hoped it might be only a few days before I would be allowed to take Steve back to Ohio. I didn't know the exact day, but my finances were running low, and I hoped we could leave soon.

As we walked to the car from the services, a deacon in a bright yellow coat called after us. "Did you get my wife's letter?"

No mail had reached me at home, so the man explained that they wanted to extend an invitation for me to stay with them the next week. God had heard my prayers. The chartered plane would drain my checking account. Here were the free room and board I would need until Steven was released from the hospital.

The twin-engine plane was a lot smaller than the 727 or DC8 that had flown me to Wisconsin and Florida. It was comforting to see a pilot and a copilot up in the front. They maneuvered the plane up and around threatening thunderstorm activity. Steven was very comfortable in a reclining seat. I leaned over to hold his hand all during the trip. It was wonderful to have my son alive and on his way home to us. God had been faithful, and very merciful.

At Burke Lakefront Airport, Steve's father waited with several of the other children. It was quite a welcoming committee. An ambulance wisked Steve off to St. Vincent's Charity Hospital for another three weeks of therapy and treatment.

He continued to make rapid progress. It was only a matter of days before he could use his legs to walk from the bed to the wheelchair. It was a miraculous answer to our prayers for his healing. I could hardly believe this miracle.

Steve's personality and happy spirit had not been squelched by the trauma of the accident. As soon as he was able, he scribbled a note to all the beautiful nurses back in the pediatric ward of the Winchester hospital to say "thank you" for all their tender, loving care.

After three weeks of occupational therapy, Steven was released from St. Vincent's Hospital. It was a joyous reunion.

Nine months later, Steven would reenter a hospital to have a piece of cartilage removed from his right knee. It was the largest piece the specialist had ever taken out of anyone's knee.

While Steven grew stronger and healthier each month, he couldn't totally escape all the aftereffects of his terrible accident. In December 1974, Steven had his first grand mal epileptic seizure. I had only a vague recollection that the doctor had warned it might happen. I was not prepared for this traumatic event. God gave me the grace and strength to survive.

9

Now that we had Steven back home with us, the plans to move out of the big house progressed in earnest. I made calls to the real estate people and then to the moving company. I could hardly believe my ears when the news reached me that the moving companies were all on strike! There was not a single company that would even furnish boxes for packing. They couldn't guarantee that the trucks would be available in July either! That meant we would be very limited in what we could move with us to Florida.

David was agreeable to driving a rented trailer behind our large station wagon. Those two vehicles would transport our linens, dishes, and a few personal items besides our clothes.

The children joined in wholeheartedly to sort through the jammed closets. Choice friends were given gifts of warm winter clothes and games. Treasures were sorted and resorted until only the best of mementos survived.

We begged boxes from all our friends. Finally, we were all packed and eager to leave for the new life in Florida. It was more painful than I expected to say good-bye to the friends who had been so loving and helpful through the long, hard times. We were treated to backyard barbecues and fancy restaurant meals. Special cakes were decorated, and gifts were exchanged. I had never known such a close fellowship with unrelated people. It was the love we shared in Jesus Christ that made us all a family such as I had never known before. Here were the brothers and sisters I had longed for all my life.

Three cars drove us to the airport. I hadn't minded selling all the furniture. It blessed me to give my nearly new refrigerator and our big, round table to the minister of a nearby church. I gave many things to Irish immigrants who had come to the area to escape the bloodshed over in Ireland. The beautiful white and gold French provincial bedroom set would thrill some other housewife. I had longed for such furniture only to find it didn't bring me lasting happiness.

As we left the yard I did not look back. The thought crossed my mind that Lot's wife was turned to a pillar of salt when she regretted leaving her home.

My ex-husband was clearly under intense emotional strain while we waited at the airport for our flight to be called. There was a half hour of small talk with friends before we could board the plane. During a lull in the conversation, he pulled me aside to ask if I had an aspirin. Waiting to say good-bye to us was very difficult. How had we reached such a point of unhappiness? Would it be worth it?

After some final kisses we boarded the plane. It was July 13, 1973.

In order for Steven to make the trip safely and without strain, he was given a wheelchair for the long walk to the gate. Since ten of us had reservations, we were seated before the other passengers. The children enjoyed this VIP treatment! I was just relieved that the seating arrangement could be transacted so smoothly.

In Atlanta, we were again escorted on the plane

before the other passengers. One of the stewardesses called me aside to ask, "Are these kids *really* all yours?" I proudly claimed all of them. What would she say if I told her there were two more of them in Florida? I had to smile.

David was planning to drive the station wagon to Florida pulling the trailer. Both vehicles were packed with our belongings. At the last minute, my ex-husband decided he would take off from his office to help David with the long drive. I was very grateful. David's father would be much more capable of driving through some of the heavy city traffic. I was sure my children's father was curious about where we would be living without him. Whatever the intentions, it is very difficult to break the ties of over twenty years as a family.

Finally, our plane arrived in Florida. As we disembarked from the plane, the heat engulfed us like a twelve-foot wave. We heard the natives complain that Daytona was having its hottest summer in years.

We moved into a motel for five days. It was a very nice place to stay, but when you are staying in two adjoining rooms with nine children, it gets hectic, to say the least. We were literally climbing over one another. The girls took one room, and I was with the boys in the other room. The motel supplied us with additional cots.

The beautiful pool was almost dangerous because of the hot sun. I didn't want the children to suffer from sunstroke.

We had perpetual picnics of fried chicken and hamburgers. Then we noticed a poster in the motel lobby offering buffet suppers. The children could eat as much as they wanted for a reduced price. The waitresses would watch with interest as my group loaded their plates. It was slightly embarrassing. They had not counted on *large* families when they offered the bargain.

We went down the street to the donut shop for breakfast. The soda we drank also took a fortune. We discovered that the tap water in Florida is never a cool refreshing drink.

I was getting a bit anxious as the days went by. The motel bill was $62.50 each night. The closing date was repeatedly postponed, and I didn't understand why until much later. In the small print of the purchase agreement is a clause that gives the buyer five days to discover such undesirable qualities in the property as termites in the house or grubs in the lawn. Being totally ignorant of such legalities, I should have been wise enough to contact an attorney of my own. Instead I was relying on the lawyer selected by the real estate people. In reality, he was working for the interests of the real estate people, not me! I will file away that lesson for the future.

The closing date was finally arranged for Wednesday noon. After 11:30, I could take my children to their new home.

My mother had been superstitious about our leaving Ohio on Friday the thirteenth. Now, as we walked into the house, I was apprehensive. The entire atmosphere of the house had changed from the first time I had seen it in May. It seemed dirty and smelly. We could take care of that, and I pushed away such negative thoughts that crept in.

David was preparing to unload our clothes from the station wagon when one of the girls screamed. Opening the hall closet revealed a three-inch-long, black, fuzzy bug on the wall. We all scurried for cover as David located the vacuum cleaner and cleared off the wall. That bug had made a lasting impression on all of us. We had never seen anything that big in

Ohio! Since every living creature has a mate, we could expect that this monster had a partner somewhere too!

It was obvious that since the former owners had planned to move, they hadn't bothered to call an exterminator for months. In Florida everyone has a choice: either have the exterminator come around for the nominal fee of seven dollars a month, or you can fight off an invasion of all types of crawling creatures. That is the price one pays for the beautiful warm climate. All things grow well in the heat and humidity.

As fast as I could I purchased new beds to get us out of the sleeping bags on the floor. We were constantly fearful of what might crawl over us in the dark. Broken screens were part of the bug control problem. When I saw the porch in May, all the screens had been intact.

Paul had a real aversion to the fuzzy creatures. Every night he sprayed a perimeter of Raid around his sleeping bag, only to find a palmetto bug or two sharing his pillow the next morning. The roaches in the kitchen drawers were harmless but obnoxious, and I never did unpack our dishes or linens.

The biggest fright for me was a three-inch spider that slid under the linoleum one night before I could attack it with a broom.

The house could have been declared a disaster area. We could not have been any more uncomfortable than we were. The boys laid their sleeping bags near the front door, just in case there was a stray breeze. There was one small air-conditioner in the master bedroom. It was no joy either! It had not been installed properly, and it leaked water profusely down the wall and over to my corner of the room.

One night I was plagued with sleeplessness, so I

wandered into the kitchen to shed a few tears alone. I got a shock at the sight of the kitchen floor glistening with water. There was a leak in the frost-free refrigerator.

The house was supposed to be of extra value because the price included a new refrigerator and the built-in stove. A repairman testified to the age of the refrigerator—four years. The stove had a burned-out front burner!

In a few days, we discovered that there was another liability in the glamorous black bathroom. The inside of the toilet tank had to be replaced. Fortunately, the real estate people knew a plumber with compassion. He came to help us the next day.

I bought a new washer and dryer for the utility room. After they were hooked up, the neighbor lady asked me if I knew that we were not connected to the city sewer. A fifty-dollar permit had been issued but allowed to expire. I felt pretty dumb, but who would guess that a house in the middle of a city still used a septic tank?

In my May visit, I had certainly been blinded by my own enthusiasm to move to Daytona. I had trusted the real estate people, when in reality, they wanted to make a rapid sale to the first easy customer. And I had certainly been eager.

I had had visions of a big garden in the ample backyard. That was until I saw dozens of lizards making their way through the grass and up the bark of the trees. Besides, the intense heat discouraged outdoor activity for the better part of the day.

We mowed the lawn late in the afternoon. We did most of our grocery shopping late in the day or evening hours. The grocery stores were open twenty-four hours a day. Elderly people carried umbrellas over their heads for protection.

Finally, after six weeks, we were all thoroughly discouraged with life in Florida. The bugs and heat were bigger obstacles than we could overcome. Our moods were constantly down, and we were miserable.

We were all spending a lot of time lounging on the beds. It seemed too hot to watch television or play games. We did more than the usual amount of praying, too. Some of us were praying to get rid of the bugs. I was questioning what purpose the expensive move to Florida had accomplished in our lives. We had implored God for wisdom for literally months before we made any of these plans. We had asked God for guidance before we selected this house! Why did everything seem so bad?

Karen came up with the most likely explanation. God had really wanted us to move to Wisconsin, but if we had gone there directly from Ohio, we would have been very unhappy the first time we had to shovel the Wisconsin snow. We would all have groaned, "Why didn't we move to Florida?" She might have hit on the right reason. I was also reminded of my willfullness in making the choice. I wasn't willing to reconsider, and God let me have my way. Now we had learned from experience that the heat and bugs were too much for us, and we could appreciate the climate up north. We could appreciate the fall colors of the trees and the cold, crisp air that stung our noses and toes. It killed off bugs too! Perhaps it was God's will that this family go back to Wisconsin.

By now it was August, and the children would have to be enrolled in school. Florida law requires a full physical examination before any pupil is enrolled in the public schools. There wasn't any way I could get doctor appointments for nine children in the remaining two weeks.

All right, Lord, we will move to Wisconsin if You can find a house for this size family at a price I can afford.

When I called my mother to tell her the new plans, she answered me with enthusiasm. Of course we could find a home in Mayville! As a matter of fact, a large duplex had just been offered for sale two blocks from the grade school and in walking distance of the high school.

Almost immediately, we felt a measure of peace. The flight plans were set for August 22. Two cars would come to meet the plane, and we would live with my mother and my aunt until the sale of the duplex was final.

That last week we were visited by a minister we all enjoyed. Perhaps if we had known him earlier, we would have been able to stay with the heat and bugs. Pastor Virgil Hull of the Flomish Avenue United Brethren Church was the kind of shepherd we had been searching for. He asked me to share my testimony with the people of the church at the Wednesday night service. When we told Pastor Hull we were leaving Florida, he begged us to stay, adding that he would pray we missed the plane!

An hour before leaving for the airport, I had to make a hurried trip to the attorney's office to sign papers authorizing him to sell the house in our absence. At a four-way intersection, a car sideswiped us, and we narrowly missed being involved in a serious accident. One of the children exclaimed, "Rev. Hull sure prays good!" We would have missed the plane if that other car had come any closer.

10

Life improved for us once we were in Wisconsin. We were in familiar surroundings near my mother, Aunt Ormenta, and old friends from my childhood. And we made new friends in church. I didn't have all the responsibility on my own shoulders, and the lighter load was more comfortable. David had stayed in Florida to live with Tommy. Neither one of them could understand why we would elect to live in the snow again, so they moved into our house to keep it safe from vandals until a new owner was found.

After I was saved, Isaiah 40:31 became personal to me. I enjoyed reading it over and over until it was a part of me. Each of the phrases had a meaning for my life: "But they that wait upon the LORD shall renew their strength; they shall mount up with wings as eagles; they shall run, and not be weary; and they shall walk, and not faint."

I had so little patience to wait for anything! I wanted things to be perfect now! When the washing machine stopped or the car didn't start, I got upset. I didn't want to wait for a total healing, I was ready now! God had different plans for me. I was impatient to be delivered from the furnace. The heat was hot! Jonah didn't like it in the belly of a fish, and I didn't like the pressure of my daily life.

Diamonds are made under intense heat and pressure, and I needed to be compressed a little. I would sit in church and plead with God for a measure of His mercy. Every sermon convicted me of a weakness or some shortcoming. The minister seemed to be looking right at me! A rebellious spirit would have led me to change churches.

The book of Job became one of my favorites. I felt like I was being tested in similar ways. Job lost his crops and his livestock. I had given up my pool and my beautiful house. Job's wife was not a help to him during his suffering. My partner was doing his best to make my life harder. I had been spared the physical problems of Job, but my mental health and emotions had certainly been tested for strength. I had been asked to give up my beloved husband to another woman. I had to watch my twelve-year-old son fight for his life after a terrible motorcycle accident. I had rebellious daughters unwilling to accept the latest circumstances in their lives. My daughters resented the new limits of a lower income, and they missed having a father.

One of my desperate needs was for masculine attention for guiding Steven's growth and energies. Help came from a young man who was willing to take Steve fishing or to an occasional ball game. It seemed like a good idea until Steve came home with unacceptable additions to his vocabulary, and worse yet, a new, more aggressive attitude. I had to be more careful in my choices of help. We didn't need the four-letter words or the added rebellion.

Pain and sorrow seemed to lurk around every corner. Several times when I waited for Mary to finish her Bible study at the county hospital, I noticed a man sitting on one of the lawn benches. His gray hair, his profile, and his body build were like my husband's. My eyes would fill with tears. The deep wounds of sorrow broke open often, and the pain was repeated.

I was born again, and in many ways, I was different and new, but in the new Gloria were still a lot of the old ways.

Jesus was real to me, and I felt His closeness. Faith and trust had to grow. It did not happen overnight. It was a gradual learning. I struggled to learn and receive love from Jesus because I needed His help. There was still a remnant of pain. There was no doubt in my mind that my help would come from Him, not from a human source.

I was struggling to make an acceptable home for my children. Every room in the old duplex needed paint and a general cleanup. Both sides had been rented out for years, and they showed it.

The first big job was to peel off layers of dirty wallpaper from the ten-foot-high ceilings. I borrowed a rickety eight-foot ladder from my mother. Barbie would stand below me with her eyes closed and her hands folded. "God, please don't let Mommy fall." Thank You, Lord, for hearing the prayers of a little child. I was finished by the time the van brought the furniture.

There were blessings to keep me going.

A letter from one of the dear friends back in the Ohio Bible-study group reminded me of their faithful prayers. Milwaukee held Jesus Rallies for inspiration. They provided spiritual vitamins to keep me going. Slowly, very slowly, the past retreated.

Sometimes my soul would soar with joy, and I lost the feeling of being earthbound.

One of these special times was on a trip to Florida to visit my two grown sons. Tom and David had come to church to please me, but after several verses of the usual invitation hymn, both boys walked forward for prayer at the altar.

My younger children had found it easier to acknowledge their need for a personal Savior. The older we get, the less likely we are to acknowledge the vacuum in our lives. We fill our lives as best we can, and we seem to be getting along as well as the next fellow. After all, doesn't everyone have problems? The world is quite permissive, and we all do some wrestling with the conviction that we are sinners.

The change in their mother was the determining factor. It was hard to argue against the source of joy and strength that they recognized as Jesus Christ. The family benefited, so they were willing to ask forgiveness and accept the gift of salvation.

After prayer at the altar, diamondlike tears rolled down David's cheeks. "I feel brand-new," he explained.

Mary and I had explained the way of salvation to Tom on more than one occasion. He was not convinced. What about all the sacraments, the holy days of obligation, all that fish and pancakes? Surely, they were of some value to a struggling mortal! No, we explained, we can't get to heaven by our own means. Jesus paid the full price of admission for us when He died on the cross. My eldest son had spent months investigating the validity of our words before he was able to walk down to the altar in submission to God's will.

I saw talent and ability in each of my children, but I am the happiest to know that they recognize their need of Jesus Christ.

The divorce was a terrible experience, but undeniably, it turned us to God. We might never have found this important relationship if all our needs had been supplied by the husband and father we adored. Now each child has been sealed by the Holy Spirit, and will worship God forever. Children born according to the will of the flesh have been given eternal life according to the will of the Spirit. We have been given a new life that will never end.

When the world speaks of God and His love for mankind, we are clearly misled to believe that love, especially divine love, means all *good* things. Surely, we think, there will be no discomfort from the hand of a loving Father. We are hurt and disillusioned when a baby dies or a young person becomes chronically ill with a crippling disease. We might even go so far as to deny that there is a God! We have trouble accepting a distorted picture of love.

I remember that my little son loved to play with a tangled mass of cords from my small appliances. It was harmless enough until I noticed him near the wall outlet. I would call him away from the danger of a shock to warn him. He had a mind of his own, and he would often ignore me. Then, I would turn him over and spank him to reinforce my words. The pain on his posterior helped him understand and re-member that my plan was the acceptable one. Could it be that God has the best plan for His chosen people? I believe that God protects us from danger.

Our trials in this world are the means God uses to mold us. I expect to be corrected whenever I get off the path to perfect happiness in heaven. That would show God's perfect love for me.

He is not without mercy. It is possible to have peace in the valley of trial. I never believed I could endure a divorce, but God was faithful to His promise to help me.

On the terrible day when Steven collapsed in an epileptic seizure, I felt the same inner strength that God had given me when this son was in a coma. The frustration of watching Steven try to put a model airplane together only to have the pieces break under his clumsy fingers was bearable, because I could expect that God was watching too. It was heartbreaking to hear Steve's poignant outcry, "What am I, a robot that has to be programmed?"

No mother stays dry-eyed under such intense emotional pressure. The difference was my ability to pray with confidence as I cried. Except for my faith and trust in God, I would have gone back to the hospital a hundred times.

Thankfully and gratefully, I have been spared the torment and loneliness of many divorcees and widows. I enjoyed being a wife and sharing the marriage bed with my beloved husband. Our closeness was almost of a spiritual nature for over eighteen years. He was everything I needed in life. He was always the dearest person in the world to me, and those memories of my husband persist. I have not forgotten love's gentle touch, the sweet surrender in a kiss, or the nearness of another's heartbeat. Yet God has quieted all those desires. He has given me this gift of grace.

The Bible says, "For thy Maker is thine husband; the Lord of hosts is his name" (Isaiah 54:5). I am content because I do not feel alone. Living life with Jesus Christ is surely the most intimate of all love relationships. He is very much like a bridegroom, and I feel like a bride when He wakes me in the night to praise Him for this new life. He wants to be praised and adored like all husbands. He is pure joy to a woman's heart. He's never too busy or too preoccupied with business. He longs to show His love for me, as the Bible says. Letting Jesus love me is the source of my joy! I hear His voice because I have a longing to get closer to Him. I can speak the deepest things of my heart, because He will not ridicule, and He is full of compassion. How many wives yearn for such freedom of communication with their mortal husbands and never receive such fulfillment!

Once I had accomplished the physically taxing job of getting the house ready for my family, I had an even harder job to face squarely. That was to raise my children without a father. At times, it seemed to be a gigantic load. I was tempted to go to bed and stay there.

Some of the same people who had been in the hospital with me had to repeat their stays. They found it impossible to gather the strength they needed to live outside the protection of the psychiatric ward. Rather than fight to live free, they gave in to the weakness.

I resented the mere hint of a possibility that I would be a repeater too, yet, I must honestly admit there were times when I was on the brink of such a decision. I felt justified in nursing my hurt pride and my broken heart.

Perhaps if I got sick enough, my ex-husband would have to assume the role of father. My bitterness was justified, but also very wrong. Only God prevented those sick thoughts from sprouting roots that would have destroyed my family. I seemed nearly helpless to raise myself from the quicksand of despair. It had to be God that pulled me out of it.

The first time I received a support check with her name printed with his, the significance of their joint checking account and their joined lives hit me with the searing pain of a red-hot sword.

I heard the story of a local woman who spent the last twenty-five years of her life in a hospital rather than live without her beloved husband who had died. That was total defeat in my mind, yet I could understand such deep pain. How tragic to hear of these drowning in the sea of despair!

Six months after we moved to Wisconsin, my fourteen-year-old daughter became very distant and rebellious. She stopped speaking to me, and she withdrew into a shell.

"It's not your fault, Mom, but I just can't live in a house without a father."

Why was she refusing to cooperate with me? I was trying so hard to go on with the business of living. Her problems seemed to coincide with another problem. Steven's epileptic attacks were very hard to control. His medication was steadily increased, and eventually his personality was severely affected. He needed more and more of my time. If I gave him all the time he was demanding, there was less and less of me for the other children. Our situation had again reached the point of impending disaster. I could not ignore Steven's problems and his need for masculine guidance. He also needed stronger discipline than I could enforce.

Struggling was the key word for all of us. I had not developed a mature trust in God. I was still trying to accomplish things on my own. My own strength was not sufficient to get me over the obstacles. In my frustration were torrents of tears. But my born-again experience had enduring qualities, and all thoughts of suicide were banished from my mind.

Occasionally I would try to smile and make a sick joke about my being the one who should have packed a bag and left. The situation was no more funny than the times I took care of a half dozen people in the throes of stomach flu. In fact, it was not funny at all, and one concern plagued me after another.

About this time, my ex-husband made plans to move to the west coast. My children and I were all concerned about the move. The children desperately needed to know that their father loved them. It would be harder to reach him over such a long distance. Here was another break in the loving relationship that had existed for two decades.

It was taking me much too long to come to grips with the fact that I did not have a husband I could depend on to help me with daily battles. My children didn't have a father to protect them from social injustice. If Steve or Peter got cheated on their paper routes, I was the adult that would have to speak up for them.

My prayers became repetitious, almost continual pleadings for divine intercession. Where was the God who took me off tranquilizers and sleeping pills in that dramatic way? It was during just such a desperate moment that my tears ceased, and a message invaded my thoughts.

The Lord was commanding me, *Stop crying. You are holding back blessings I have for your family.*

The tension and pressure of the long months were lifted immediately. What joy! God was not deaf or distant! He was with me, and I had His strength and help for the battles.

The next Sunday night I virtually ran up to the altar at prayer time. Tears of cleansing coursed down my cheeks. I would relinquish all claim to my own life. I prayed, "Dear Jesus, You rescued me from eternal death. Now wash me clean of all those undesirable things I still harbor in my heart. Fill me with Your Holy Spirit, and take control of my life."

I had received the Holy Spirit in April 1972; now the Holy Spirit received all of me. I turned over my will to God. I resolved to be His obedient servant to the best of my ability. I would listen for His guidance. I would let the Bible speak to me, and I would seek the fellowship of other Christians so that He might speak to me through them.

It was only a matter of weeks before the blessings of God came as He had promised.

Steven's problem was difficult to handle because he didn't feel different. I went to the school, a psychiatrist, and then a neurologist to get professional opinions. At last, on the advice of these professional people and with the help of a social worker, I had to concede that the best solution for Steve and the other children was a residential treatment home for him.

I have not forgotten God's ability to take a brain lesion away. He is still the miracle-working God of the Bible. In the meantime, we found an excellent residential treatment home for Steven. After an interview, I was satisfied that my son would receive the best possible care and help from a well-qualified staff. Drugs were controlling the seizures. Most important, as time went on, Steven's attitude changed from offensive aggression to an acceptable attitude of consideration and love for his brothers and sisters. When they deliberately provoked a fight with him, he had learned to restrain himself. Previously, the smallest incident would send him after them in a rage.

As a very human mother, I prayed God would take away the lesion on his brain. I prayed for an end to the terrible epileptic seizures that were so painful and traumatic, but I have learned to wait on the Lord. I have learned not to argue with God. I cannot understand His wisdom in letting bad things happen, but then I have only limited human insight. Perhaps Steven has a ministry at the school he must attend. As the house mother unpacked his suitcase the first day, she said to him, "You must be a Christian. You aren't like the others." More than one boy or girl has been helped because Steven has a great capacity to *feel* for the pain of others. He has a sensitivity and maturity that would put some adults to shame. I have peace knowing that God understands I can't provide the structured life

Steven needs to become the person he will be for the glory of God.

My rebellious daughter went to live in a Christian home for a year. Concerned friends from our own church were willing to be licensed as foster parents to help us. Occasionally, our families could get together on a holiday or celebration. We were able to keep in close touch.

I had serious financial concerns when my ex-husband moved to California. He would be earning less, and we were to cooperate by accepting less alimony and child support each month. I was proud of the way the children had responded when we were giving up the big house and the beautiful pool. They had doled out their private possessions to friends when we moved into a much smaller house. Their bravery was stoic! No one raised an objection to giving up those material possessions, but now there was a threat to the money we needed for the essentials. A gnawing insecurity would wake me from my sleep. I had accepted a job as a preschool teacher's aide to supplement our income, but since I was classed as single on the tax forms, I made very little financial progress.

The day of the court hearing to reduce the payments, my attorney called me. He seemed very concerned, but suddenly I felt reassured that everything would work out satisfactorily. I didn't pray for help, as in the past. Instead, I said, "Thank You, Lord, for all the love You have shown for this family." We won both the first hearing and the appeal case. It was further confirmation of God's loving care for this family.

I found I would wake from a sound sleep with a happy spirit instead of fear and apprehension. I felt as if I were wrapped in a security blanket of God's love. I felt a new expectancy—not of adversity, but rather,

"What do You have for me today, Lord?" I could feel His strength when my own legs would have trembled with weakness. Fourteen pills a day never had given me that kind of peace.

Now I understand the truth of the last part of Isaiah 40:31: "They shall walk, and not faint." Most of life is not traumatic or even dramatic. Life can be like a level landscape; just an hour-by-hour, day-by-day happening. We need the quiet times to recover and recuperate. Time like that is never dull if the believer has made an attempt to see God in all things. Mundane events can be colorful and even exciting times to praise the Lord for His goodness.

One day I listened to a minister telling his radio listeners that it might be to our advantage to take Jesus Christ along to the grocery store in these days of inflationary prices. That sounded interesting. Perhaps I had finally reached the degree of Christian maturity where I could listen to all spiritual advice.

I remembered that suggestion one day as I pushed the door open and reached for a grocery cart in the store. The ladies of the church had planned a bake sale, but I was very low on grocery money. I had the choice of baking something that did not require flour, or I could pretend to the others that the bake sale had slipped my mind. My conscience did not approve of the latter choice, so I counted the change in my purse. *Lord, I really need Your help if I am to bake for the sale.* Midway down the second aisle, there stood a cart loaded with packages and boxes of damaged merchandise. Here was a bag of the flour I needed—just fifty-seven cents! *Thank You, Lord.*

One fall our linen closet looked pretty bare. Six fitted sheets had succumbed to the wear and tear of the years. Remembering the incident with the flour, I decided to talk to the Lord about some new sheets.

As I walked through the department store, there stood a table piled high with slightly irregular sheets. They were just two dollars apiece! I was able to purchase six sheets of the proper size for just twelve dollars! I felt light and happy all the way home.

I believe that kind of attitude can keep the believer from "fainting" as he walks through life. As conditions worsen in the world toward the days of the Tribulation period, we must look to God for all our needs. Those of us who can turn back from seeking luxury and pleasure of the world are most likely to survive with whole minds and bodies. We will find delight in the small pleasures, the simple things, the natural things God will surely provide.

I could see God in every circumstance of my life, even the day I nearly got a ticket for speeding. That may sound illogical to some, but there was no doubt in my mind.

I had just visited Steven six weeks after he left home. My mind began to race over the tragic events that had forced me to place Steve in a boarding school so far from the rest of the family. I was lonely for Steve, and he was miserably homesick. I felt sad enough to cry, and I didn't have my eye on the speedometer. I was on the verge of being very bitter for circumstances I couldn't control. Suddenly, I was conscious of the flashing red light of a squad car. I pulled over to the side of the road while tears welled up in my eyes. *Yes, Lord, I know this is Your will for my life. The divorce, the motorcycle accident; all of it is in Your divine plan.*

I opened the car door and walked back to where the officer was marking down my license number. I blurted out, "I'm sorry." Through my tears I saw the kindest face, and he was smiling at me. I could hardly believe it, because I deserved to hear some pretty harsh words. Instead, he handed me a warning ticket, and said very little about my infringement of the speeding laws.

He seemed like one of God's angels that stay near us to help us avoid impending dangers. I sincerely believe this "angel" stopped me from speeding toward the wrong attitude as well as toward physical danger.

I believe there was another "angel" in human form sent to spare me untold misery. In my early days of depression, I confided in a neighbor. I didn't know the woman very well, and she was usually at work, so it was rare to see her in the backyard. As we visited about our children and our husbands, I confided to Kay that sometimes I considered taking a drink a half hour before my husband came home. It was painful to see him slowly drag himself out of the car and reluctantly enter our home. Perhaps a small drink of wine or brandy would take the edge off my distress.

Her face stiffened with alarm. "Oh Gloria, please don't do such a thing. You would become an alcoholic in no time with that attitude," she warned me. Her words persuaded me that alcohol was not the answer I needed. Now I shudder to think how close I came to adding to the tragic events of my family.

My Christian growth has been a slow process, but I realize that a child coming out of kindergarten is not ready to graduate from college. I know that my upward climb has been a carefully guided tour around sand traps or through them, as my own free will dictated. I needed much refining before I could begin a life of obedience. I know that the learning process will continue as long as I live, but perhaps the lessons can become a little less painful as we go on to Zion.

When death takes a father, it is a clean wound that finally will heal. Divorce leaves a dirty wound that can fester with guilt and self-condemnation. Further disease will result if the lives are not changed and cleansed.

Some authorities on the subject recommend group therapy. Because I had to have the state's assistance with two of my children, it was suggested that I attend a group therapy session each week in the fall of 1975.

What a sad group it was! There was a sense of faltering struggle to regain respect for the individual and for others. Each of the members was to talk about the previous week's struggle with his job, family, and particularly, encounters with members of the opposite sex.

One slightly built, moustached male was quivering with doubts of his masculinity. His second wife had just left him with five young children. He wanted to find a girl friend, but he had grave doubts that any female could be trusted.

A girl in her early twenties was pathetic. She came from a large family. Her sisters had all married well, and she had been anxious to find a mate. Unfortunately, she had not made a wise choice. The husband abused her and their small children, so a divorce had to be arranged. The girl had fled home to her mother.

The mother had a severe heart problem and died soon after. The girl could not face a second loss. She spent several afternoons each week literally clinging to the mother's gravestone.

The bushy-haired man next to me was determined to get pleasure out of life one way or another. If one woman had left him, there was sure to be another that would find him appealing. His plan to test his virility and masculine appeal was to approach a likely candidate and ask her to sleep with him. If she said yes, then the previous divorce was not his fault. He gave no thought to the guilty conscience he might have to live with after the tryst.

I surveyed the group and listened with interest. They were not finding cures. They were taking all their dirty laundry to a public laundromat, but they didn't bring the cleansing agent! God had washed me of sin and guilt. How could I share that and at least plant a seed that might sprout faith in the weak little man, the torn heart of the girl, the guilt-ridden Don Juan. Jesus can heal broken lives and hearts if only we come to Him. As we were all required to take a turn at sharing, I used my turn to give my testimony of God's power in my life. The counselor commented that I had an "interesting" story.

Satan doesn't let the Christian alone. There were times when bitterness, self-pity, and even hate could have found fertile soil in my heart. What woman wants to be left with the problems of coping with eleven emotionally upset children? When the problems were real, or when my maternal instincts were overreacting, there was no husband or father to consult or sympathize. Neighbors were very kind and helpful, but frequently they fanned the flames of discontent by offering me a generous amount of pity.

Why was it necessary for the minister to join me at the hospital for hours during some crisis? Where was the man who had fathered these children? It took inner strength to fight off the attacks. Instead, I would will myself to pray, *Thank You, Lord, for this good friend who is willing to wait with me.*

My lifeline to God was constant prayer. Not because I was commanded to pray, but because Jesus was fast becoming my dearest friend and confidant. I could turn to Him in loving obedience and never be turned away.

Christian fellowship made my days much brighter. God faithfully directed my path to people who could help me with the tremendous responsibility of being a single parent to nine children. There were always "angels" along the way to encourage me and lift my faltering footsteps. One man took his daughters for a rowboat ride on the river, and there was always room for some of mine. When Steven was bursting with the energy of a growing boy, the minister found time to pass the football or play a game of tennis. When my daughters struggled with the rebellious spirits of teenage girls, this man left his own daughters to counsel mine with understanding and firmness.

When the children were all babies and my husband would be gone on a week-long sales trip, I would often be tempted to collapse with emotional and physical fatigue. After a week or two of doing the job alone, I was very happy to have my partner take a turn at parenthood. Now I have been the single parent for years, not just weeks. There is no way to explain my strength, my energy, my outlook on life, except to give Jesus Christ the credit for all that I am or hope to be in the years before me. I truly have been "crucified with Christ: nevertheless I live; yet not I, but Christ liveth in me: and the life which I now live in the flesh I live by the faith of the Son of God, who loved me, and gave himself for me" (Galatians 2:20).

11

I have been inspired by many Christian books. When I read numerous testimonies of faith, I realize that *their* God is *my* God, and He offers me the same help that He gives to others.

I read about new love in the midst of a broken marriage. I read inspiring accounts of people who were tortured and imprisoned for their faith. How was it possible for an invalid to give a joyful testimony? Obviously, it is not what happens *to* us that is important, but what happens *in* us! It is the presence of God that makes adverse circumstances bearable—even joyful—experiences! How is that possible? Jesus Christ merely demands that we look to Him for the solution. We must be pliable to become what He has planned. Do we suffer because we give up our will? Of course not. God has a plan that is good, but it is not necessarily one that we would choose.

"This plan of mine is not what you would work out, neither are my thoughts the same as yours! For just as the heavens are higher than the earth, so are my ways higher than yours, and my thoughts than yours" (Isaiah 55:8, TLB).

My favorite Bible verses are those that tell about Jesus appearing on the water late at night while His disciples were in a boat:

"And in the fourth watch of the night Jesus went unto them, walking on the sea. And when the disciples saw him walking on the sea, they were troubled, saying, It is a spirit; and they cried out for fear. But straightway Jesus spake unto them, saying, Be of good cheer; it is I; be not afraid. Peter answered him and said, Lord, if it be thou, bid me come unto thee on the water. And he said, Come. And when Peter was come down out of the ship, he walked on the water, to go to Jesus. But when he saw the wind boisterous, he was afraid; and beginning to sink, he cried, saying, Lord, save me" (Matthew 14:25-30).

Of all the men in the boat, Peter was the only one to have the courage to step out onto the water. It appears to me that I have often been like the other disciples. It took me quite a while before I could see Jesus in everyday circumstances. How many times have I lacked the courage to step out in faith, and trust God to be in my situation? We cling to our humanness, and strive to solve the problems in the ways that seem best to us. After we fail a few times, we fall to our knees and implore God for the help He has made available to us from the beginning.

Peter could walk on the water as long as he kept his eyes on Jesus. When he looked down at the waves lapping at his feet, he panicked. When Satan sends a wave of fear or anxiety, I falter. It seems easier to worry than to pray! How earnestly we should pray for the faith to look to God every day, in every circumstance. We could avoid so much pain. My grandmother knew how to "walk on the water" in her hardships. What an example she set for me.

In 1975, my eldest daughter, Karen, enrolled in a Christian college in Springfield, Missouri. That is about six hundred miles from our home, so we planned that Karen would fly down in time for the opening of school. Once all the paperwork and preliminaries were completed, we began to pack her belongings. Paul had just left for his first year at Moody Bible Institute with a small amount of baggage and his stereo. As Karen set aside all the things she would need, it became quite obvious that her plane would have difficulty taking off! Boys travel without two dozen shoes, long dresses, electric curlers, and all the things that Karen could not live without. Well, as I thought about it, there was really only one solution. I would have to drive down to that school in Missouri. It would be a long trip, but Karen could help drive, and I would take a leisurely trip back home. My aunt agreed to be my companion on the long trip back home. I forgot how apprehensive I had always been to drive on a freeway or turnpike. I always needed to draw strength from the husband who was seated beside me.

I made the necessary arrangements without mental debate. I was finally learning to take one step at a time and not be limited by worry. It was going to be a busy holiday weekend, and I could have a flat tire, but that could happen right here in Mayville! I prayed that God would give me the necessary skill, but the rest was placed in God's hands and left there. Nothing would happen to us that God didn't allow for a good reason.

We loaded the station wagon until it was groaning. There was room for just one passenger in the back and two of us in the front. The weather was slightly overcast, but that was a blessing, because the brighter sun would have caused eye strain.

When we arrived in Springfield it seemed a good idea to do some sightseeing. The school did not open its doors until late on Sunday. A glance at the map showed us that Tulsa, Oklahoma was just two hundred miles away. We had already driven six-hundred miles in one day, so another four-hundred miles on Sunday didn't seem like too much. The heat and humidity were oppressing, but we had undampened, adventurous spirits.

I come from such a long line of people who hesitate to step out in faith, believing something good *can* happen! One dear lady still talks about the successful potato chip business she might have had. She had all the required cash, and she even had customers lined up, but she was afraid to take that step of faith. An uncle could have had a booming floral business. His gardens attracted people for miles. I always teased him that he could make a board grow roots. But he was afraid to take the step of faith.

I have resolved to stop limiting God in my life. The Bible says, "Ye have not, because ye ask not" (James 4:2). I have learned that there is no limit to what God will give His children if they trust.

Oklahoma was as hot as Missouri, but my heart had a song in it. Suddenly, on the Will Rogers Tollway, the silly thought came to me, *What's a nice girl like you doing so far from home?* Was God teasing me? It was a long time since I thought of myself as a "nice girl"! I enjoyed a sense of release right there with all the cars speeding around me, and the heat pressing in on us. Dripping wet with perspiration, I felt like sixteen again.

We got back to Springfield Sunday evening, and now we could carry all the belongings up to Karen's second-floor room.

On Monday, we rested in the air-conditioned motel room. The temperatures were in the high nineties, and the humidity was equally high. In the evening we had to dress up for a vocal concert at the college. The barracks-type building that serves as the chapel was like an oven, but the vocalist gave a beautiful testimony in song, and we forgot our discomfort.

Early Tuesday morning we filled the gas tank and

left for Wisconsin. The heat was getting worse. Cows stood under trees hoping for some relief. Whenever possible they stood knee-deep in water.

As we got closer to St. Louis, I began to think about the six lanes of traffic. There was a busy expressway around the city. I tried to build my confidence by thinking about the trips I had made to downtown Cleveland the weeks that Steven was in the hospital. I had hit the busy rush-hour traffic every day.

My palms were red and slippery on the steering wheel. The car felt the heat too. The wheel felt like it was greased under my hands. I gripped it with all my might. I grew more tense as the traffic increased. I decided to ask God for a measure of His peace and comfort.

As I glanced to my right toward the horizon of tall buildings, my eyes caught sight of a beautiful white dove. I could hardly believe it! God's peace sign put out there just when I was desperate. I saw it two or three times before we had driven too far.

The balance of our trip was remarkably easy. I didn't feel stiff or weary from driving six hundred miles since morning. The trip had been more than seventeen hundred miles! Quite a distance in three days of travel for a reluctant driver like me! I sat back to consider the goodness of the Lord. I had obviously been healed in body, soul, and mind. Nothing is too hard for God. The Bible says, "Heal me, O Lord, and I shall be healed; save me, and I shall be saved: for thou art my praise" (Jeremiah 17:14).

Now I felt equipped to begin a new life. All the fear and hesitancy that held me back was gone. In 1971, I couldn't convey my thoughts in speech. I couldn't write my name or read a newspaper. God has given me abundant life with the divine command to live.

By Christmas 1975, I began to think seriously about

reentering college. A small private college just twenty-six miles away accepted sixty-nine of my seventy credits for transfer. That was such a miracle, I felt it must mean a green light of approval from above. Again I searched my heart. There were still five children at home to take care of every day. Would I neglect them if I had homework of my own every night? God had blessed me with eleven beautiful children, and I surely needed to give them top priority. Would the school involvement turn me into a carnal Christian as I became more and more absorbed with academic achievement? These thoughts led me into earnest prayer that God would always remain as close as He had been so far in my experience.

Wisconsin had its worst winter of blizzards and ice storms. As I left home for my classes every day, I frequently found the highways unplowed and slippery. After my last class, the afternoon shadows made the drifting snow look very menacing. I sang all the hymns and choruses of praise I could remember. I prayed and looked to the magenta sky for encouragement. The daily trips became precious times alone with God. Jesus went to school with me, down the halls and into the classrooms.

My children's father came to visit us for a few days in February. We had not been on very good terms since he lost his bid to have the support payments reduced. I debated with myself. Should I go to the trouble of cooking a dinner, or would he prefer to take the children out to eat, and thus avoid sitting at the table with me?

A few days before his visit, I was chatting with a friend about grain shipments to Russia. I did not understand all the economic implications, but I voiced the opinion that it seemed to me that we should feed all the hungry people here and in friendly countries first. This lady replied, "The Bible says love your enemies." The message came through loud and clear. I knew I was supposed to cook a dinner for our visitor. The Bible tells us we must forgive and turn the other cheek. The grace of God has kept me from being bitter. Early in my years of turmoil and pain a good church-going friend suggested I "shoot him in the head and watch him bleed." I was aghast, filled with horror at such a pronouncement. Perhaps I retain so many beautiful and good memories of the man. More likely, by the grace of God I see what a hopeless sinner I was until God pronounced my pardon. Slowly I see my faultless prince becoming an individual capable of weakness and mistakes. The concept is much more realistic than the one I treasured for all the years of our marriage.

I prepared a dinner of his favorite foods. He responded by fixing a leaky faucet washer for me and a flat tire on one of the bikes. The visit was a happy occasion for all of us.

He came again in April for the staff meeting with the people from Steven's school. Once more, Steven had the loving concern of *both* parents.

Easter brought beautiful weather, but problems and pressure began crowding my pleasant thoughts. It was a dry time in my spiritual life. The pressure of final exams and my role as a mother and housekeeper were becoming heavy again.

One evening I went to bed early for a retreat period with my Lord. I longed for the closeness that had given me strength and comfort so many times before. I stayed awake until I had prayed for all the children and their needs. I praised God for the beautiful way He has cared for each of us. Our needs had often been met in a miraculous way. I finished, and waited for sleep to overcome me. Suddenly, I was jarred back to full consciousness. Across my brain flashed a vivid message, "TRUST ME." It was in capital letters like a neon sign.

The next thing I knew it was morning. I had hoped to wake up refreshed, but I never expected to feel this degree of rejuvenation and refreshment. I floated through the next few days. I went to class and wrote the final exams without effort. There was no more anxiety as I left the results with God.

The next big event was Mary's graduation from high school. We had planned a small celebration supper. We invited my husband's parents, my family, the minister and his family, and a few good friends. Twenty people crowded into the dining areas, but the mood was relaxed and happy. The food stretched to accommodate a few extra people, and it seemed everyone had a happy time. Mary and I rejoiced at the way the Lord had removed all fences and dissensions.

I was scheduled for a complete physical exam on the following day. I was not worried, but I felt it would not be unusual for the mother of eleven to develop some problems by age forty-eight. If the Lord granted me a few days rest in the hospital, He would have good reason for doing so.

Just before I left for the doctor's office, the mailman arrived with my final grades from college. Opening the envelope was exciting. I had put out a fleece. *If* God wanted me to continue with the studies toward a degree in elementary education, I would expect higher-than-average grades. I had before me a 3.5 grade point average—two B's and two A's. Those were excellent grades from a college with high standards. I was singing praises to God for restoring my mind.

The doctor had all the results of my tests and examination before him on the desk. He leaned back and grinned at me. I had shared the good news of my grades with him. Now I heard him call me a "terrific lady"! I found it hard to be comfortable with such generous praise, but he was obviously quite sincere. He went on to tell me that I was unbelievably sound. He wouldn't expect me back until next year.

I felt bathed in love as I drove home. The doctor's praise echoed in my mind. "You are a terrific lady," he had said. Where was the ordinary housewife from Ohio? Well, I wasn't ordinary anymore! I felt very special, and John 15:16 verifies my position as a chosen one of God.

Ten years ago, a friend stood at my elbow while I turned out bacon and eggs for a room full of eager eaters. She watched my expertise and exclaimed, "Gloria, you should write a book!"

That was an ego-fulfilling thought, and I smiled at the prospect. I could have turned out a volume on how to raise your children to be well-mannered, respectful, and straight. Better yet would have been my book on how to fill every moment of the day with useful activity. The reader would have belched efficiency as the thought of the amount of work I had to do prompted indigestion or a preulcer condition. I did not subscribe to much leisure or relaxation. My busy life-style would have made a firmly packed edition.

This book has been an attempt to spread the good news of Jesus Christ as seen by a *new* Gloria Hurst. Furthermore, I want to sell you on the idea of having a personal relationship with Jesus!

I've seen your faces lined with anxiety and disappointment. I want to tell you there is a better way to live.

You may have gone to church for years, but you come home still empty and lonely. Perhaps you don't bother going to church. You may be at the point where you don't care if you hit the bottle or your wife, hate your boss or love your neighbor's wife. You overeat, or overdress before the idol of materialism.

Sin comes in all shapes and colors. You may not be in the black pit of despair, as I was. You may just feel frustration or emptiness. When Adam took a bite of the fruit, the entire human race got sick. We are helpless to overcome our burden alone. I enjoyed being told my great-grandfather was one of the founders of a local church. I had gone to church nearly every Sunday of my life, but I was hopelessly trapped and doomed to spend eternity in hell. None of us is good.

Jesus released me, and He is waiting to give you the same total healing and a new life. Give Jesus a chance to change your life. He stands at the door of your heart and knocks (Revelation 3:20). You open the door to Him simply by acknowledging your need to be saved from sin. The sinful nature of man separates him from God. We cannot understand how our sin was laid upon Jesus, but God says in His Word that it was. Jesus literally died in *your* place! His blood that dripped down from the cross washes *you* clean. What a tremendous gift—free, unearned by any of us. We receive God's pardon the moment we take God at His word, and by faith we claim salvation—freedom from sin and life everlasting.

You may not feel a dramatic change in the morning as I did. Don't depend on your feelings. If you have prayed sincerely, believe you have a new status in life. You are now a child of God with all the rights and privileges. We have become "joint-heirs with Christ" (Romans 8:17). There will come a day when you feel special, and it will be glorious!

There are some helps necessary for spiritual growth. First, you should learn the habit of praying. Prayer is a natural conversation with God. Don't be hesitant or shy. He knows you from before you were formed in the womb. Be honest with Him. He reads your heart.

Second, get a Bible that reads to your liking. There are many editions on the market. Some are in modern English that is very easy to read. Pray before you read, and God's Word will unfold before your eyes. You may be surprised to find that you will understand the Bible quite easily.

The third help to your Christian growth will be fellowship with other Christians in a church of your choice. Look around until you find a church that teaches and preaches the Word of God as changeless doctrine.

One of the first indications of a new life in Christ may well be that you begin to enjoy the services. You may have been a steady churchgoer, who left the services with the same empty feeling that he brought. Now you hear the message with new ears, and the dullness is gone. The pastor's message may prick you—even bring tears of resentment to your eyes. That is the Holy Spirit convicting you of some area that needs changing. Listen with an open and willing spirit. God is speaking to you. Other Christians will welcome you in a spirit of genuine love. Ask God to help you love these new brothers and sisters in the Lord. You will experience such joy that you will want to tell everyone you meet. I am praying this book has encouraged you in this way.

Since 1972, I have been living in an aura of God's love. I doubt that mere words have done an adequate job of expressing the beauty and the excitement of the experience.

I grew up thinking of God's love as a giant blanket over the entire human race. In these years I have come to understand that His love for me is very personal.

There are four billion people living on the earth at this time. As a child in Sunday school, I was impressed with the Bible verses that tell us God clothes the lilies of the field. He knows when a little sparrow falls to the ground. How much more tenderly does He view His children?

Recently, the state of Wisconsin experienced a terrible ice storm. Three days after the storm, I had to drive through the countryside. The fields were still covered with ice. They glistened like silver lamé in the sunshine. Then I noticed something quite remarkable. The grass wasn't covered by a giant blanket of ice. No, each blade of grass had an individual coating of ice. There could be four billion blades of grass in just that one field!

God's love is like that ice. He has the ability to give each life a personal touch, and I know He yearns to do that for everyone that asks Him for this blessing. The abundant life of gifts and power for this life comes from a constant desire to have an ongoing relationship with God.

My family is a miracle of God's grace. He was so tolerant with us during those years we lived a "good" life by our own wits and abilities. Seven years ago He stirred our nest. We could have remained in the world and resented His chastening. Twelve of us chose to accept His plan and live by His grace. None of us has decided to go back to the old way of grim survival.

We live with the assurance of the abundance of His love, the sweetness of His joy, the comfort of His peace, and the security of His strength. Praise the Lord!

Moody Press, a ministry of the Moody Bible Institute, is designed for education, evangelization, and edification. If we may assist you in knowing more about Christ and the Christian life, please write us without obligation: Moody Press, c/o MLM, Chicago, Illinois 60610.